"Joan's story is very moving and well-told. Since cancer touches so many lives today, I feel that this book will be of great interest to a very large number of people who, like Joan and Mark, are looking at what alternative healing can offer and asking the deeper questions about life and death."

—**Norie Huddle**
Author of *Surviving: The Best Game on Earth*

"Joan Peterson relies on a higher power to help us witness the challenges she and her husband confronted in his up-and-down bout with cancer. The journey is sometimes exhilerating, sometimes painful as this devoted couple tests the limits of alternative medicine and healing practices. Their common goal to find solace guides them toward inner harmony and peace.

Regardless of your spiritual beliefs, you will be moved to embrace the wisdom that Joan and Mark find through their poignant struggle."

—**Carolyn Kreiter-Foronda, Ph.D.**
Author of *Contrary Visions* and *Gathering Light*

Love Has No Fear

One Couple's Search for Healing

Love Has No Fear

One Couple's Search for Healing

Joan Peterson

Merkaba Press
Falls Church, Virginia

Although the author and publisher have made every effort to ensure the accuracy and completeness of information contained in this book, we assume no responsibility for errors, inaccuracies, omissions, or any inconsistency herein. Any slights of people, places, or organizations are unintentional.

First printing 1997

ISBN 0-9656017-5-7

LCCN 97-93355

Editing, design, typesetting, and printing services provided by About Books, Inc., 425 Cedar Street, PO Box 1500, Buena Vista, CO 81211, (800) 548-1876.

ATTENTION HOSPICES, CARE GIVER ORGANIZATIONS, AND HEALTH CARE ORGANIZATIONS: Quantity discounts are available on bulk purchases of this book for educational purposes. Special books or book excerpts can also be created to fit specific needs. For information, please contact Merkaba Press at P.O. Box 6511, Falls Church, VA 22040, (800) 673-6056.

Dedication

This book is dedicated to the memory of Mark Peterson,
my husband for thirty-five years
and my best friend.

And to our daughters, Teresa and Kristen,
who walked with us on this journey,
shared the daily struggle,
the joys, the tears.
They are enlightened souls and I'm forever grateful
they chose us as parents.

Acknowledgments

I am deeply grateful for the constant support and encouragement of my daughters, mother, sisters and brothers, and extended family members. I also wish to thank Mark's sisters and their families for their love.

I especially want to thank friends who read the original manuscript, encouraged me to publish and gave helpful suggestions: Jean Whitman, Susan Trout, Carolyn Foronda, Dorien Israel, Gary Bietz, Milde Waterfall, Linda Morris, Ann Goutreau, Jayn Adina, Sallyann Poinsett, Stan and Shirley Scheyer, Bonnie Peed, Leslie Jolley, Elliott Dacher, John White, Carol Parish, Gordon Davidson, Ken Nelson, Ruth Hornbaker, Carolyn Carlyle, Jean Boston, and Cindy Cox. I am particularly indebted to Merrill Whitman for his help in editing and to Norie Huddle and Peggy Millin for their manuscript critique and tireless assistance in editing.

Elisabeth Kübler-Ross, Stephen Levine, Ram Dass, Gerald Jampolsky, Joan Borysenko, Larry Dossey, Bernie Siegel, Carl Simonton, and Herbert Benson, among others, all speak of new possibilities in working with the seriously ill. I am grateful for the wisdom from their teachings that I was able to apply to our experience.

Preface

Love Has No Fear: One Couple's Search for Healing is the poignant yet never-depressing story of Joan Peterson's husband's death from renal cancer. It is a story for the critically ill and their caretakers who struggle with the choices among contemporary medicine and alternative healing approaches. We know that positive thinking, laughter, and visualization can heal the most deadly diseases—*but* it doesn't work for everyone, and where it doesn't, guilt and feelings of failure usually result. *Love Has No Fear* takes us on one couple's quest for healing, illustrating how critical illness provides an opportunity for family members to heal old wounds, to deepen their love for one another, and to grow spiritually even though the growth may take very different paths. The most refreshing aspect of this book is that it does not provide any answers to choice of treatment or why a given person survives the same disease that kills another. Instead it opens doors to life's great questions about death, immortality, and the meaning of love and of "forever."

—Peggy Tabor Millin
Author of *Mary's Way*

Foreword

Mark Peterson taught me the most important lesson
left to learn in my life—how to die with dignity.
I am grateful to Mark for so many things
during the twenty years of fun and friendship we shared,
but none more than this: I now know how to die.

I watched Joan, his wife and my spiritual mother,
as her love, will, and wisdom
kept Mark with us on this planet
longer than anyone thought possible.
But in the end I saw her do the most loving thing of all—
she let him go.

Joan and Mark showed me the importance
of the yang of living well
and the yin of
letting go.

—**Dorien Israel**
Author, *Tao Passages: The Way Home*

—

Contents

Foreword xiii

Introduction xvii

Chapter One: *Weekend Cancer* 1

Chapter Two: *Reprieve* 9

Chapter Three: *More Questions than Answers* 17

Chapter Four: *Cancer Strikes Again* 25

Chapter Five: *Rallying Resources for an
Uncharted Journey* 33

Chapter Six: *Energy, Attitude, and Food* 43

Chapter Seven: *Visualizations, Meditations, and Humor* . . 53

Chapter Eight: *Black Thursday with Western Medicine* . . . 63

Chapter Nine: *Spiritual Calm and an Emotional
Roller Coaster* 71

Chapter Ten: *New Hopes and Old Fears* 85

Chapter Eleven: *Macro-Mellow Mark* 95

Chapter Twelve: *Bittersweet Days and Dreams* 101

Chapter Thirteen: *Another Kind of Cancer
Treatment Begins* 111

Chapter Fourteen: **Stressed Out and Angry**   117

Chapter Fifteen: **Struggling Against Depression**   123

Chapter Sixteen: **Dreams and Remembrances**   135

Chapter Seventeen: **Countdown to Eternity**   145

Chapter Eighteen: **The Sacred Vigil**   155

Chapter Nineteen: **Memorial Services**   165

Chapter Twenty: **Life Goes On—Forever**   175

Epilogue   183

Resources and Books   185

Introduction

When my husband, Mark, discovered he had kidney cancer, a particularly deadly form of cancer, the shock and trauma was tremendous. Since traditional Western medicine offered little hope, we sought our own path of healing. Thus began a journey of unusual spiritual experiences difficult to understand within the mainstream world view. During the darkest hours, spiritual phenomena confirmed there was a divine plan in progress. It gave us courage to continue, even though we did not know what lay ahead.

Besides the awakening to a higher level in his spiritual life, Mark's fine analytical mind had to admit the alternative healing approaches—attitudinal healing, meditation, Reiki healing, imagery, macrobiotic diet—made him feel physically better than he had in many years. He observed that despite having cancer, his *quality* of life had improved greatly. And he lived with cancer for *years*, not *months*, as one doctor had forecast.

When he finally started western medical treatment his sense of well-being deteriorated dramatically due to the side effects of the treatments. A rocky period ensued, fraught with emotional highs and lows. The seriousness of Mark's condition deepened the level of intimacy and understanding in our family as we gradually reached the stage of acceptance. We had been inspired by many books about cancer survivors, but now at this stage—where were the books about those, who like Mark, had tried everything we could think of and still did not receive physical healing? I wanted to learn how others coped—but I found very few books telling this story.

Even as Mark's physical condition worsened, his sense of humor and courage remained intact. He told me that dying was an "interesting process" and he began to design his funeral—considering making a tape that began, "Unaccustomed as I am to speaking at my own funeral . . ." We became telepathic with each other and strange phenomena occurred with more frequency.

Mark died at home in his sleep, almost six years after his diagnosis. He died with dignity and grace.

I did not intend to write a book. After my husband's death, grief weighted me down, and to relieve the pressure I began to sort and sift through memories of our life, spilling them down on a yellow legal pad. Writing became a major part of my healing process. My daughters, Teresa and Kristen, added their thoughts and insights, which gave us an opportunity to talk, laugh, and cry together as we reminisced. When I finished, the weight had lifted. But did I dare share such personal experiences with friends and family? Many times Mark taught me to face fear, so with trepidation I did . . . and it was their encouragement that led to this book being in your hands. I share it with you now because I realize we are not strangers . . . we are all one.

The startling simplicity of the statement, "You are not a physical being having a spiritual experience but a spiritual being having a physical experience," caused me to exclaim, "Why, of course!" Life before death, death, and life after death are all part of the same mysterious spiritual continuum.

Death is part of life. It touches everyone. The next time you are in a crowd, look around . . . one out of three people you see will have cancer. This book presents many questions about the origins of illness and both traditional and alternative treatments. It offers comfort to people struggling with life and death issues, not because it gives answers, but because it empowers them to make their own choices and find their own truths.

This is a love story, a story of healing into life, into death and beyond.

Proceeds from the sale of this book
will be used to provide dolphin experiences
for children with cancer.

Chapter One

Weekend Cancer

"Joan, I think we have a problem."

I opened my eyes and blinked at the sunlight streaking in through a gap in the drapes, promising another hot day on the Chesapeake Bay. My husband Mark and I were in the aft cabin of our boat. I had been enjoying the delicious state on the edge of sleep, lulled by the boat's gentle movement and sounds of water lapping against the hull. But the strange tone in Mark's voice sent a shockwave of apprehension through me. I bolted upright and scrambled across the bed, the shortest route to the head. Mark stood silently looking down at the toilet bowl. It was filled with dark red blood.

We stood there looking in disbelief. What was going on? My big, strong, six-foot-three-inch, two-hundred-pound husband was not sick. He had no symptoms. Only fifty-five years old, Mark was the picture of health, tanned and robust. My mind raced. What should we do now? We did not have a family physician or even know the location of the hospital closest to our marina at Herring Bay. Mark suggested we look in the phone book for a urologist in the area.

"No, we should drive to the emergency room of the nearest hospital," I said. "Any urologist will probably send us there for tests anyway." My logic won, and we were soon in the emergency room at the hospital in Prince Frederick, a small town fifteen miles away.

The doctors inserted a catheter, examined him, and took X-rays. Before releasing him, they asked Mark to urinate. He discovered he couldn't. Apparently there was some blockage, so he stayed for more tests. Finally, after setting up an appointment with an urologist for the next day, we returned to our boat.

Our tiny pocket poodle, Poozie, met us at the sliding glass door to the salon, racing back and forth, jumping on and off the couch in sheer joy. Her display of unconditional love was more exuberant than usual. Poozie knew from our abrupt departure that morning something was very wrong.

The rest of the day passed quietly without either of us talking much about the morning's events or even daring to think too much about the possible diagnosis. Unspoken and unshared, the C word—cancer—lurked in each of our minds.

The next day Mark wanted to go to the doctor's appointment alone. When he returned, I knew the news was not good. I was preparing for a workshop I was to present the next day in St. Louis. Mark sat down opposite me in the dining booth off the galley. He said, "The scan showed shadows in the right kidney." Trying to soften the blow, he added they weren't positive it was cancer; more tests were scheduled the next day. We both grasped onto the small uncertainty as a glimmer of hope; perhaps it was just kidney stones.

"I'll cancel my flight and go with you for the test," I said.

"No," said Mark. "There's nothing you'll be able to do anyway because I'll be in the hospital for most of tomorrow. I'll be fine. Besides you'll be back from St. Louis by tomorrow evening."

I didn't want to leave, but with Mark's encouragement, I flew to St. Louis. I somehow managed to present my workshop by pushing my concern for Mark out of my mind. The moment the session ended, all the worries came flooding back. I raced to the airport to catch the first flight back to Washington, D.C.

The hour drive from National Airport to the boat seemed to take forever. When I arrived, I knew something was wrong. The boat was dark. The moment my foot hit the dock, Poozie went wild, barking and scratching at the door. I let her out to run, but in record time she shot back inside. She threw herself at me with such intensity, I knew she had been alone a long time.

Where was Mark? His car was gone but there was no note. Then I saw the light blinking on the answering machine. "Hi! I'm at Georgetown Hospital," said Mark's voice. "I'm having a party in room three thirteen. Why don't you come join me?" No other explanation. It was so like Mark to make light of the situation.

I called friends in McLean, Virginia, to ask if Poozie and I could stay with them and grabbed my Rolodex. My unpacked suitcase was still in the car. After dropping Poozie off with our friends, I went straight to the hospital. I felt things were spinning out of control. This couldn't possibly be happening to us.

Mark was remarkably upbeat as he described his day. While I had been in St. Louis, Mark experienced severe pains in his right kidney. He bypassed the local hospital and the scheduled invasive test, picked up his X-rays, and made an appointment with a specialist at Georgetown Hospital. He began the hour-long trip doubled over the steering wheel with pain, but as he pulled up to the hospital, the pain subsided. After one look at the scans, the specialist announced, "The kidney needs to be removed; the tumors are ninety-five percent certain to be malignant." The operation was scheduled for the next day.

That night I telephoned our immediate family, contacting our daughters first, Teresa in Florida and Kristen in Charlottesville, Virginia. How do you prepare children for the shock their dad may have cancer? Wanting to protect them, I said something inane like, "Now don't worry. Everything is all right, but Dad is going to have his kidney removed tomorrow." Then I called Mark's two sisters in Seattle and my mother and family in Minnesota, not just to inform them, but to ask for their prayers. I knew about well-documented research on the positive effects of prayer on a patient's recovery and I wanted Mark to have all the prayers he could get.

I didn't sleep much that night. Everything was happening so fast I hadn't time to get used to the idea that the next day Mark would be cut open and his kidney removed. What else would the doctors find? How far had the cancer spread? What was the prognosis for people with renal cancer? Toward morning as questions swirled around and around, my mind drifted back to our wedding day thirty years ago.

"Try your luck!"

The barkers' entreaties joined laughter of the crowd and music from the carousel as I spun around and around on a Ferris wheel, trying to hold down the hoop of my satin wedding gown. The soft, warm breeze created by the motion of the ride caressed my face. I breathed deeply the contrasting fragrances of sawdust, cotton candy, and farm animals at my hometown county fair. It was August 23, 1958, and I'd just married Mark. I was eighteen years old.

My childhood was spent on a farm outside of Herman, population five hundred, in western Minnesota. I was the youngest of ten children. In high school, I was a "big frog" in a little pond.

Mark and I met at Macalester College when I was a naive seventeen-year-old fresh from the family farm. He was a worldly ex-marine, seven years older than I, going to school on the GI bill. He and his buddies in the Vet Club seemed to party a lot.

We were both active in the speech department. That fall we went on a bus trip to Wisconsin to participate in a speech and debate competition. Mark and his debate partner won first place. On the bus ride back to Minnesota, a group of students needed another person to play the card game Hearts. I volunteered and found myself sitting next to Mark. We talked and laughed the rest of the night.

The next day Mark called to invite me out that evening. I have a weak eye that was very bloodshot from staying awake the entire previous night so I didn't want to go. But Mark was very persuasive; we went out for pizza. Several months later he told me that he knew he had fallen in love with me then, red eye and all.

Unlike many of my friends who dreamed about getting married, I planned to have an exciting career. I was going to live abroad and travel around the world. Getting married and settling down was the last thing I wanted to do. I didn't even want to get serious with anyone. How was I to know then that in less than a year I'd marry Mark and move to Seattle? Or that later, I'd finish college, have a career, have two children, live overseas, and travel the world. I got everything I wanted and more!

It was as if some huge invisible magnet pulled me inexorably toward Mark and the altar, even while my head argued I was too young to be married. I'd just discovered the big pond and was starting to become a big fish in it, too. I would be giving it all up and moving far away from friends and family. I loved Mark with all my heart and wanted to be with him forever. Even so, I dragged my feet all the way to our wedding.

To celebrate our last night as singles, Mark took me out along with his best man and one of my close high school friends. A nondrinker, I found myself downing with wild abandon several sweet Tom Collins, perhaps trying to still the nagging voice of uncertainty that I felt about our pending marriage. Much later that evening Mark walked me up and down the road so I could vomit. At that point I wouldn't have blamed him for questioning whether he really wanted to marry me, either. On my wedding day, I woke up grumpy and with a bloodshot eye—just like on our first date. So much for being a typical fifties-style sweet blushing bride!

After the marriage ceremony, which Mark's father performed, my brothers and their friends kidnaped me. They hoisted me onto their shoulders, wedding dress and all, and carried me away to the fairgrounds and put me on the Ferris wheel. The operator got into the swing of things and after letting everyone else off the ride, kept me going around and around, up and down.

A cheering crowd gathered. As I swung down I gazed with fondness at the people I'd known all my life, and as I rose to the top of the ride I looked out over my little hometown and said goodbye—then looked out further to the horizon and beyond. Around and around I went. The ride cleared my head; as I looked out into the distance, peering into the unknown on this warm summer evening, I suddenly became very eager for my new life to begin. Something deep inside me told me quite clearly I was meant to be married to Mark.

The Ferris wheel operator finally let me off the ride and my brothers brought me back to the reception. Mark hugged me. "Hey, I knew they'd bring you back," he laughed.

Now Mark and I were on a strange new ride together. Facing the unknown, I longed for the big view from the top but I couldn't see it. Thoughts spun around but always bogged down on Mark's operation the next day. As I finally fell asleep, I wondered when this ride would end.

At five o'clock the next morning Kristen arrived, her eyes full of concern. She had spent a restless night too. We went immediately to the hospital to be with Mark. When the attendant came for him, Kristen and I walked down the hall beside Mark on the gurney. The nurse stopped us at the door to the operating room. A quick kiss, a few whispered words of love, and Mark disappeared behind the doors, leaving Kristen and me clinging to each other, neither one of us daring to speak.

Numbed by a feeling of unreality, we walked into the waiting room and gave our name to the volunteer receptionist, who encouraged us to go outside for a walk or get something to eat. It would be at least two hours before the doctor could give us a progress report. We took her advice and ate although we were not hungry. When we returned to the waiting room, we still had to wait for what seemed like an interminable time. I tried to meditate, but my "monkey mind" jumped from thought to thought, wondering what was happening to Mark.

Finally, the surgeon came and introduced himself. The operation had gone well. Yes, Mark's tumor was malignant. No, it looked as if the cancer had not spread beyond the kidney. I had been hanging onto the slim chance that the tumor would be benign, that it would be one of the five percent not cancerous. I felt the word "malignant" hit me like a physical blow as it echoed over and over in my brain. The surgeon's face remained expressionless throughout his explanation. When he finished talking, we just looked at him. Kristen later said, "I wasn't expecting a 'high five' or anything, but maybe a smile, a pat, or a 'he did great.' "

By the time Mark returned from the recovery room, I had assimilated the bad news and was concentrating on the good. The first thing I told him was, "They got it all." Mark was groggy and in a great deal of pain. The nurse promised, "As soon as I get you settled, I'll give you a shot for the pain." Mark smiled weakly and said, "Great! Make mine a double with lots of ice." The nurse seemed a bit taken aback. Kristen and I had to smile. Not even cancer could dampen Mark's sense of humor.

After Mark had been given his shot and I knew he would sleep, I told him I was going to the hospital cafeteria for a bite to eat. He looked at me from half-closed eyes and said, "If I were you, I wouldn't order the kidney pie for a few days." At a time when I felt most like crying, I couldn't help laughing.

Mark recovered from surgery in record time. The doctors released him only three days after the operation. We'd gotten off the wild ride and went back to the boat to heal. We walked. We watched sunsets on the Chesapeake Bay. We were thankful the ordeal with cancer was over. Or so it seemed. When friends asked about his operation, Mark replied, "Yes, I had cancer for a weekend."

Chapter Two

Reprieve

Grateful for the reprieve, we realized how precious life was and drew closer together. Mark was a pragmatic doer whereas I am more reflective and intuitive. Politically we were in opposite camps; the same was true about our views on social issues such as welfare and prison reform. Perhaps his experiences as a drill instructor in the Marine Corps influenced his tough line approach. Mark loved to debate; I wanted to dialogue. So we agreed to disagree in these areas and didn't discuss them much. Yet we made a strong team, bringing balance into each other's lives. Over the years I gathered a rich and often amusing reservoir of personal examples of how a couple can have the same experience yet perceive it so differently.

At a crossroads professionally, we were thankful to have this free time to be able to plan for the future again. Mark's "can do" spirit had made our life interesting in the past.

After college Mark and his brother-in-law formed a business to manufacture and market their own inventions, such as a free-standing fireplace, a space heater for campers, and a pop-up tent. I began teaching elementary school.

Two years later, our daughter Teresa was born. We'd sit and gaze at her, agreeing she was the most beautiful marvel we'd ever seen. Mark worked long hours at his business and was shocked when I once remarked, "You may not realize this, but it has been three weeks since you have seen Teresa awake." That shook him up, and he made the decision he did not want to miss out on her day-to-day development. So, after three years of running his own business, he shut it down and went to work nine to five for Boeing to help design its SST prototype. After Kristen was born in 1966, Mark left Boeing to work in airline management. We moved to Taipei, Taiwan, for three years, when Teresa was four and Kristen a year and a half.

The girls grew up next to a Buddhist Temple thinking it was quite routine to ride on the back of my moped between rice paddies, attend Chinese opera, and have a maid who let them suck on fish eyes. To Kristen and Teresa, funerals were a source of entertainment—a loud, colorful procession with truckbeds full of people singing. Flowers covered many types of carts that were pulled, pedaled, or motorized. Marchers with decorated faces and masks followed horses wearing masks while acrobats performed stunts. Bands played *Jingle Bells* and *How Dry I Am*, any tune with a good beat it seemed. I thought the funeral celebrations appropriate and perhaps even more fitting than our mournful rituals. The unfortunate commonality was the expense: families often went into debt to pay for the lavish sendoff. It made me ponder a Confucius quote, "While you do not understand life, how can you understand death?" My world view expanded as I observed different religions in action.

Exploring a new culture was exciting, and I was mostly unaware of America's turmoil during the late sixties. I became inured to the Vietnam War. It was all around us—Taipei had an active military base and soldiers came to Taiwan for rest and relaxation. We didn't have television and without stateside coverage, I knew little about the war or the growing protests at home. I often joined Mark on trips, and once he took me water skiing on the Saigon River. Even though I could hear gunfire in the far distance, it seemed a normal thing to do until he cautioned, "Watch out for bodies floating in the water."

Early in the 1970s, we moved to Virginia, and for several years led busy lives raising our children and expanding our careers. Around age fifty, Mark found his work no longer satisfying and decided to take early retirement. In 1984 we sold the lovely home we had built in the woods outside of Oakton, Virginia. Profit from this sale enabled us to become gypsies for the next several months. We moved aboard our forty-two-foot trawler and prepared for a cruise south down the inland waterway.

Mark had a way of plunking me down in the middle of physical danger and the first day of our voyage was one of those times. It's said we get to experience what we need to learn—I guess I needed to learn to face fear. We began our journey confidently cruising out into the Chesapeake Bay one crisp November morning with steaming cups of coffee in our hands. An hour later, we faced a raging storm. At the helm, Mark wrestled with the wheel in a tense crash course in how to handle our boat in the seven-foot waves. He quickly got the hang of it, whooping and hollering with glee as the boat rose onto the crest of a wave only to surf down the other side of it into a deep trough. "Can you believe we picked up almost ten knots of speed coming down that wave?" Mark chortled.

Meanwhile, I clutched Poozie under one arm and clung to the railing for dear life with the other, paralyzed with fear, muttering relevant passages of the twenty-third Psalm under my breath, over and over, "Yea, though I walk through the valley of the shadow of death . . . ." A sense of peace would flow into me for a short time; then another panic attack would hit, and I'd have to repeat the whole process. Later I scribbled in my journal:

> *The gift of fear—*
> *how precious it is*
> *as it leads me*

to my edge.
Face to face
smiling in acknowledgment,
naming it by name—
"fear."
Only then can this
now named offspring of the mind
lose its power and pain.
Just as I lose happiness
by grasping it,
I am free of fear
by greeting it.

Nine hours later we docked at Tides Inn, on the Rappahannock River. Contents from the refrigerator had flown all over the cabin, plants had crashed, spilling dirt on the floor, the television and tape deck had toppled off the shelf ripping out cords. What a mess! We went for dinner at Tides Inn Restaurant, but I was too emotionally drained to enjoy the lovely meal. Mark, on the other hand, ate heartily.

I didn't want to go back out into the storm the next day. In fact, I thought it would be lovely just to stay at the Tides Inn forever. Mark convinced me by saying, "The weather is only going to get worse so we'd better go now. In a couple of hours we'll be in Norfolk, and then we'll be in the protected Inland Waterway." But as we headed back into the Chesapeake Bay, the waves were just as high as the day before. "Oh no, I need to 'greet' fear again," I thought. Looking down at the roiling, surging seas as we were tossed about, with wave after wave slamming relentlessly against our boat, I felt sick. It was then I discovered a truth that has helped me many time in other life situations. Instead of looking down at the angry waters, if I kept my eyes on the horizon, focused on the vision of where we were headed, I could handle the storm. A "couple of hours" turned into eight before we finally docked in Norfolk.

Once we actually got on the protected part of the Inland Waterway, the trip was wonderful, a unique view of quaint fishing villages and wildlife along the coast. It was a treat to pull up along side shrimp boats to buy our dinner fresh from the sea. We cruised for six months around the Florida Keys and the Gulf of Mexico. Whenever we had engine trouble, often in very secluded areas like deep in the Everglades, Mark somehow was always able to fix it.

Some friends said they thought selling our home and taking off like we did indicated a mid-life crisis. We called it a mid-life opportunity. It seemed like a great time for an adventure. Both of our daughters were now involved in college life, and we had avoided the usual empty-nest syndrome by selling our home. Our girls were the only ones at the university whose parents called *them* collect. They thought what we were doing was pretty cool and joined us wherever we were for holidays and spring break.

Since we were not independently wealthy, when we returned to the Chesapeake Bay in April 1985, we both needed to explore new careers. After my year's sabbatical, I decided not to return to work as coordinator of programs for gifted education, which I had been doing for seven years. Instead, I decided to concentrate on my sideline consulting business with school systems, businesses, and government agencies, focusing on lifelong learning. I also decided to get a masters degree in human resource development.

I became involved with friends in creating a nonprofit, spiritual learning center in Washington, D.C. Our opening workshop was a weekend with visionary psychologist, Jean Houston, and world renown mythologist, Joseph Campbell. What a dynamic duo! When we said goodbye and thanked Joseph Campbell, he said, "No, I want to thank you. I needed to do this again." I believe it was his last large group workshop before his death. It was an exciting opportunity to meet people like them and, through the center, others whose work I admired.

After our six-month cruise, Mark decided to build houses for his new career. He designed a house and set out to build it, hiring one carpenter to help him. He lived in a tiny sixteen-foot trailer during the week so he wouldn't have the long commute back to the boat each day. He called his trailer cozy and didn't mind having to haul water from a friend's house nearby to fill his water tanks for showers. I stayed on the boat, out of his way, but would sometimes go out to visit and see the progress he had made on the house. I was amused to discover I could mop the trailer's living room, dining room, kitchen, and bath without moving my feet if I stood in one place and swivelled.

Building a house gave Mark many opportunities to exercise his creative problem-solving mind. The house was a large contemporary out in the country near Manassas, Virginia. When the house was completed, we camped out in it during the winter months getting only what we needed from our things in storage. In 1986, we sold that house and bought a bigger fifty-foot boat. We loved living on the water, and I decided to offer seminars afloat. We named our new boat *Contentment*.

It was during this period of living aboard *Contentment*, in the summer of 1989, Mark had his bout of "weekend cancer." After his surgery and speedy recovery, a friend asked him to oversee the building of a shopping center in Stafford, Virginia. It was a long commute from our boat, but Mark would leave later in the morning and return early in the afternoon to avoid traffic on Interstate 95 and the beltway around Washington, D.C. He really enjoyed the building process. Mark loved to see the tangible results of his labor.

Cancer taught us to not put off making decisions if there was something we wanted to do. We decided to buy a house in Punta Gorda, Florida, to spend the winter months. Winter on a boat with snow and ice is cozy, but we both preferred warmer weather. We looked at several houses and even tried to talk ourselves into buying one of them, but each time something wasn't right. We were about to give up the whole search when, driving back to the motel, Mark said, "I feel like we should just drive down this street."

We turned the corner and drove down one block, and there it was: a beautiful Spanish-style hacienda, and it was for sale. We both knew it was ours. We drove straight to the realtor but she told us it had already been sold. "Are you sure? Please check again," I said. To her surprise and our delight, she discovered "our house" had just come back on the market. We knew we wanted it even without seeing the inside.

We learned from a neighbor that dolphins used to swim by frequently, but few had been sighted during the last several years. Ever since I first encountered the ocean, I have felt a powerful connection with dolphins, so I started a quiet little experiment. In my mind, I imagined I was talking with dolphins. "I love you," I'd tell them. "Please swim up our canal and visit me." And we started seeing quite a few dolphins. After awhile, I became confident enough to tell my rational, practical Mark, that I was going to ask them to swim by, and then we'd watch to see if they appeared. Quite often they did. Even our neighbor commented how unusual it was to see so many dolphins in the canal.

We rode our bikes each day exploring Punta Gorda and making new friends. Mark was in great shape and easily rode fifteen to twenty miles a day. Grateful for Mark's miraculous recovery from his weekend cancer, we treasured our time together. The romance in our marriage also rekindled, burning brighter than ever as we both realized we should never take each other for granted. We were like honeymooners, laughing and loving every day. Cancer teaches many lessons.

Chapter Three

More Questions than Answers

Mark's bout with cancer renewed my search for answers about the meaning of life. For many years I'd searched for a relationship with God that went beyond the confines of the traditional Christianity of my youth.

I first started questioning religion as a young girl. One dreary winter day, riding home from school on the bus, I had a sudden "knowing" that my father was in the hospital and would never be coming home again. My premonition proved true; my father died when I was fourteen. It was a turning point.

Our minister preached, ". . . if you smoke, drink, or work on Sunday, you'll burn in hell." Yet Dad occasionally enjoyed a cigar, a beer, or a shot of bourbon. On Saturday nights, our whole family would go into town. While mother visited with friends as she did the week's shopping, the men went to the pool hall. When it was time to go home, we kids tapped on the forbidden pool hall window and Dad would come out. He never emerged drunk or evil; he had simply relaxed with friends after a long week of hard work on the farm. And, if the crops needed harvesting on Sunday before the weather changed, he worked on Sunday too. Once when I asked, "Daddy, do you believe in God?" He paused and reflected. "I don't believe I could be a farmer if I didn't. Every time I plant a seed, I believe."

But if the minister was right, my father was definitely headed for hell. At his funeral I decided that kind of religion wasn't for me. Besides I'd also observed that some of the most pious and faithful church members were busybody gossips, and I really didn't want to end up in heaven with them anyway.

So I left the church at that young age even though my physical body still attended dutifully with my family every Sunday. But my spiritual journey had just begun. There had to be more to religion than all the arbitrary rules for getting into heaven, punishment, and damnation. What about all the other religions in the world? Could there be one God and many paths? I wanted a loving God rather than one I had to fear. Growing up with nature, I felt the presence of Spirit and it felt like total love. I didn't see how it was possible to love and fear God at the same time.

Life overseas expanded my world view. But life became a whirl of activity and travel, without my taking many moments for quiet contemplation. It wasn't until I was in my thirties that a growing dissatisfaction drifted into my life. On the surface of things, I had everything. My husband cherished me and provided for our material needs; our daughters were healthy, intelligent children; I loved my career. Actively involved in school, church, and community activities, we also cared for three foster children; a Vietnamese foster daughter lived with us for almost two years. I felt productive and useful but somehow it wasn't enough. In the 1970s, open marriages were in vogue, but I had enough sense to realize the problem wasn't with Mark or our relationship; it was within me. There had to be more—but what? What was the real meaning of life? What was my mission?

My search for answers began by examining the world of psychic "signs and wonders." A couple of fellow teachers and I were introduced to this world at a Consciousness Frontiers conference. We sat on my back deck afterwards to discuss the concepts of psychic phenomena, precognition, and mind over matter. I voiced my concern about appearing weird for being interested. "I am relieved the people at the conference all looked normal." Still, I was glad I had not met any of my students' parents there. Not feeling able to articulate my growing belief in unlimited potential, I wasn't ready to come out of the closet yet. However, the new information on precognition helped explain why as a child, I often knew things before they happened.

It also made me feel better when I heard astronaut Ed Mitchell, the sixth man to walk on the moon, say, "There is no such thing as the supernatural. It is super and it is natural. We just have very wide gaps in our understanding of it." He founded The Institute of Noetic Sciences to study the mind and diverse ways of knowing. I joined.

A new world of possibilities opened as I learned views of reality different from my own. After hearing psychic healer Olga Worrall speak, I took friends to a healing service she conducted. A friend's tumor disappeared, enabling her to avoid surgery, and the arthritis in her fingers vanished. A serious buildup of fluid in the ears of another friend's eight-month-old daughter cleared when Olga held her.

As a child, Mark too had struggled with the "do's and don'ts" of religion. His father was a Baptist minister, and it was difficult being an active little boy who had to sit still during three full services every Sunday. When he left home, he no longer attended church. But his strong belief in a divine power opened him to the acceptance of these miraculous healings.

He didn't join me in my spiritual search for answers to the questions "Why?" and "How?" He'd say, "Some things just are. I don't need to know why." His interest, I discovered, only went so far. Still eager to share, I returned from my first Spiritual Frontiers Fellowship retreat exploring psychic phenomena and mystical experiences. "We studied energy and pyramid power," I told him. "We even put metal pyramids on our heads to experience the energy."

"You wore pyramids on your head?"

"Yes," I babbled, "and then we all sat inside a large pyramid to magnify the energy out on the lawn!"

Amused, Mark raised his eyebrow. "You mean you actually went outside wearing pyramids on your heads?"

Ever practical, Mark thought my new experiments and explorations weird. In retrospect, I can see why, although he was intrigued when I learned I could bend forks and spoons with my mind. And he listened intently without comment when I recounted how a psychic, whom I had just met at the retreat, said she saw a motherly figure in spirit who was showing three paralyzed fingers as a means of identification. Mark's deceased mother had three fingers paralyzed from a car accident. The entity said she was happy to see Jean with Mark's dad and that she had helped. (Mark's ninety-two-year-old father had just married eighty-six-year-old Jean.) To show her love, the motherly figure was giving us a bouquet of blue flowers. Mark and I were on our way outside as I finished telling him this and when I opened the front door, there on the doorstep was a bunch of blue flowers. I have no idea where the bundle of blue flowers came from—we lived in the middle of five wooded acres. Could it really be possible to communicate after death?

I found I could discuss ideas about biofeedback and meditation with our friend Stan, a physician. I'd given him books such as *The Relaxation Response* by Dr. Herbert Benson and *The Turning Point* by Fritjof Capra. Stan, who was very interested in these new concepts, began practicing meditation and was soon an advocate. His acceptance as a physician of the power of the mind in health and healing affirmed my growing belief that through our minds we have greater control over our physical health than modern science admits. While Stan and I shared our discoveries, Mark and Stan's wife, Shirley, usually carried on their own conversation in another room. We didn't know then what an important role Stan would play in helping Mark deal with cancer later on.

I never really discussed metaphysical concepts with Teresa and Kristen. When they were older, I figured they could decide for themselves. However, they witnessed the benefit of my daily meditation practice. The girls knew that during this twenty-minute gift to myself, I was not to be interrupted unless the water in the kitchen reached chin level! They observed that I lay down after work exhausted and rose refreshed, invigorated, cheerful, ready to cook dinner, help with homework, and take them to play practice or softball games.

Although Mark didn't share my interest in esoteric philosophy and metaphysics, he couldn't ignore the healing of my rheumatism. This particular event was a transforming experience, and I still feel joy whenever I think about it. On the way over to a meeting held for the purpose of contacting guidance from higher spiritual beings, I told Spirit, "If I am to believe in any of this stuff, I want to experience some phenomenon myself tonight."

An intuitive counselor led the session, and soon others in the group saw visions and heard voices. Everyone, it seemed, except me. Until the end of the session. Then slowly a powerful electric current pulsated up my hands and feet, growing stronger and stronger as it traveled up my arms and legs. It was like I was holding onto an electrical livewire. The electric current pulsated so strong I could not bend my fingers. My body faded and I became pure energy. At the same time I felt total bliss and love, at one with the universe. This was what I had been searching for!

Mark was asleep when I got home, but when I told him about it the next morning he said, "Too bad it didn't cure your rheumatism," a condition I'd had for many years. Then it dawned on me. I had no pain in the knees! I had been so excited about the totally blissful experience I hadn't realized my pain was gone. After that incredible experience, which left me permanently healed and feeling high for months, I never had to accept divine love on faith alone. I knew it to be true because I'd experienced it.

This spurred me on to study Reiki healing. Reiki, an ancient Tibetan spiritual healing method, gently balances the mind, body, and spirit. Literally translated, Reiki means "Universal Life Force." After taking the training, a group of friends and I offered Reiki healing, without charge, once a week for seven years at Jean and Merrill's home. Jean and Merrill had become my spiritual mentors of sorts. After silent meditation, we usually worked in pairs on anyone who came. Each session took about an hour and almost everyone felt a wonderful flow of energy and healing love.

We witnessed several miracles. My skeptical mind wondered if the healing could be a placebo effect or the simple transfer of our own energy, rather than energy from a divine source. My questioning was partially answered when a woman I worked on whenever she came, reported that the color blindness caused by childhood measles had disappeared. She was so unaccustomed to seeing colors that she had ceased to think about it. On full disability retirement, she had come for Reiki in the hope of relieving other physical problems. The cure couldn't be a placebo effect if she wasn't focused on it and we didn't know she was color blind. In addition to this healing, she was able to reduce her insulin dosage for diabetes from eighteen units in the morning and seventeen units in the afternoon down to just twelve units. Her blood pressure dropped from 200 over 120 to 150 over 80.

Often I was so tired in the evening I didn't want to make the effort to go to the "Ashram on the hill," as I called Jean and Merrill's charming old country home. But after the healing sessions, I'd be full of energy and well being. During those seven years, I never had a headache, a cold, or the flu. As I helped others, I helped myself.

Another fascinating topic emerged. Kenneth Ring and Raymond Moody wrote books about people who had died and returned to life, filled with wonder at what they had experienced on the other side. When I shared my readings about these near death experiences with Mark, he surprised me by saying, "I've done that."

When he was twelve, he was in a very bad car accident with his parents and aunt. His mother and aunt were taken away first in the small town ambulance. He remembered hearing the attendant say, "We'll take them first; the kid's gone anyway." The top of Mark's head had been cut open and he was left by the side of the road for dead. "I remember walking up an incline along a path with high dark banks on each side, like a tunnel, toward a beautiful, bright meadow I could see in the distance." He knew it was a most wonderful peaceful place, and he wanted so much to be there. He didn't quite get to go to the top because he heard his father's voice calling to him. "I didn't want to return, but decided I should do it for my father's sake." His father had crawled out of the wrecked car and was by his side as Mark returned to consciousness. Thinking his experience unique, he had never shared it. It explained to me why Mark never seemed to fear physical death, why he loved adventure and living on the brink.

Accounts of near-death experiences raised many questions in my mind about life after death. After reading *There is a River*, Thomas Sugrue's book about Edgar Cayce's life, I read everything I could find on the subject of reincarnation. Ian Stevenson at the University of Virginia and other well-established researchers have written very persuasive studies, especially with research involving young children, in support of reincarnation. Reincarnation made a lot of sense to me because it helped explain how a just God could allow babies to die in famines or to be born defective. If a soul gets to choose its life experiences for a reason, even though not easily understood on this level, life then appears to be more than just the "luck of the draw."

I also found particularly persuasive such cases as those reported in *Mission to Millboro*, in which groups of people discovered, under hypnosis, interlocking past lives. In this book, people living on the West Coast told of an underground room in Millboro, Virginia, used to hide runaway slaves during the Civil War. When researchers followed up on these reports, they discovered the room. Until then, no one in Millboro knew it was there.

If reincarnation is not an explanation for such knowing of the past, then there must be something even more complex and wondrous going on. When we remember a past life, are we making contact with the shell or a fragment of a soul who once lived—this fragment still existing on the astral level? If many people contact the same fragment, could that explain why many claim a past life as Cleopatra or other famous people? Or if time is relative as Einstein said, could we possibly be living past, present, and future lives simultaneously in different dimensions of the universe? If we really are all one on the spiritual level, could a past life memory be from tapping into that shared oneness? Pondering these spiritual matters, I ended up with more questions than answers.

Meanwhile, wanting to cover all bases, we took our daughters to the Methodist Church. I didn't want to give up religion, just expand it into spirituality. Later, when the girls were in high school, we discovered a Unity Church, which welcomes all denominations. I immediately felt in tune with the philosophy of inclusion and lack of dogma.

Because I had been on a spiritual search for many years, when Mark got cancer, I relied on faith that there is a divine plan for each of us. But what was the divine plan? Had Mark and I agreed on the soul level to be together again this lifetime? If so, what lessons did we need to learn from each other? Why cancer?

Chapter Four

Cancer Strikes Again

The two years after Mark's kidney operation passed quickly. They were busy, happy years. We spent our winters in Florida, with friends and family coming to visit, and the hot summer months living on our boat on the Chesapeake Bay.

Despite general good health, Mark was often bothered by indigestion and gas pains. Doctors at various times labeled it hiatal hernia, diverticulitis, or it seemed when they didn't know what else to call it, irritable bowel syndrome. Although they didn't suspect cancer, they finally decided to do a CAT scan of the stomach area. The tips of Mark's very long lungs showed up in the scan as well; the doctor thought he saw something in the right lung. More tests confirmed that the cancer had indeed metastasized. The doctors recommended immediate surgery to remove sections of the lobe of Mark's right lung.

Once again everything went into high gear. Should Mark have surgery? Doctors told us the tumors were small; surgery was the best chance to keep it from spreading. It was an easy decision for us. We wanted to get the cancer out of his body! Surgery was scheduled that week.

Mark was the "strong silent type." I thought it was important for him to express his emotions as he recovered from his second bout with cancer. I gave him notebooks, drawing paper, pens, and paints. He chose not to paint, but he did keep a journal.

7 June 1990

It is difficult to describe in exact terms one's feelings about preparing for major surgery on the day it is to take place. Getting up, showering, shaving and all the regular routine things that one normally does each morning are all overshadowed by the constant thought that in a few hours, you are going to be on an operating table with a surgeon actually cutting into your body. This makes for an unreal sense of time and being as you watch the minutes slip away.

Fortunately the day itself was beautiful and as Joan and I left the boat I couldn't help wondering, as I looked across the quiet marina and out to the bay, whether I might be viewing these all for the very last time. The same held true as I drove to the hospital— was this to be the last time I experienced slow traffic or riding in a car with Joan? This was not necessarily a negative or down feeling but rather one of wondering whether this might be the start of that great unknown journey that all of us are going to experience one day. I felt perhaps the early explorers felt this way as they began their voyages into the great unknown—excited yet apprehensive.

With unusually light traffic, we arrived at the hospital so early that we went into the cafeteria so Joan could have breakfast and I could watch her eat it. While Joan ate, I watched a group of medical students having their breakfast and couldn't help wondering if, in several hours, any of them would be observing my body being cut open and whether during this procedure, any of them would give any thought to what they had for breakfast. Again, the breakfast routine took on an unreal feeling regarding the use of time and it was almost as if as long as we kept on doing other things, the inevitable wouldn't happen.

Actually entering the main hospital building gave me the first feeling that the surgery process was underway and that there was no turning back. Checking in and preoperative procedures were routine and all were well designed to "put you at ease." My pre-op physical and interview were done by a third year med student who went out of his way to assure me that everything would be okay. Joan was able to be with me through all this and her presence was very comforting even though I felt like an actor playing out the scene that was expected of me.

I brought a subliminal tape with healing words recorded beneath the easy listening music and I asked if it could be played during Mark's operation. We were told that the doctor played music he liked. When I expressed concern that I hoped they would not say anything negative during surgery that Mark's subconscious would hear and remember, possibly affecting his recovery, he assured me they were too busy for idle talk during surgery.

The next major item was the nurse coming in to announce that they were on their way to bring me to the operating area. The time between this announcement and the gurney actually arrived was one where I knew I could still get up and walk out. I kept wondering why people don't do so rather than just sit and wait for the ultimate to happen. Part of the good actor bit, I guess.

Placing one's healthy, whole body willingly on the gurney is the final act of total submission to the process and logically makes no sense as you know that in a few hours, this same body will be turned into one totally painful being. Being wheeled through the halls and down the elevators is very unreal, as you know that you are perfectly capable of walking, yet you are now only a part of a play whose direction is totally out of your control. As you pass other people, you wonder what they are doing and whether they have any idea what you are about to undergo.

Now comes the point in the journey where Joan is told she can accompany us no further. A quick kiss and a brief clasp of hands before we go our separate ways. Again the question arises: "Will you ever again see this woman who means so much to you?" Or, "Will this last glimpse of her standing there have to last you forever?" Strange, but at this point I couldn't help wondering what she would do if I didn't survive. More specifically, I wondered how much trouble she would have dating again and who would eventually take my place with her.

Once again I sat in the waiting room, trying to use the time to plan a workshop on humor to present the following week. How incongruous to be planning a session on humor while Mark was in surgery! Two friends joined me later for the long wait since Teresa and Kristen were both living in Florida.

Next stop, the preparation room. Here you join the others who are waiting for the various operating rooms to be prepared to receive them. You lie there and watch; one gurney after another is rolled away. Sometimes you catch a quick glance of a face of someone you have never seen before and will probably never see again; yet, in that brief instant you seem to establish an unique type of bond, a bond between two individuals who, among all the people in the world, are about to undergo a very unreal, and for most, a very frightening experience—the final journey into the unknown.

The anesthesiologist stops by to ask if I am allergic to certain things, to give a brief description of his part of the operation, and to tell me what to expect. He also describes what I can expect upon awaking, what extra equipment I might find attached to my body. Finally, he tells me not to worry as I am in very good hands.

Dr. Gomes stops in to chat briefly. He asks how I feel. My reply is that my feelings are not the important issue but what is important is how does he feel? A laugh from him, a quick handshake, and a parting, "I'll see you in the operating room."

A period of waiting follows. I realize I can still get out of what is coming if I really want to. I do nothing. While waiting, one realizes again and again just how unreal this entire procedure is. Here is a room full of people just waiting for a lot of painful things to be done to their bodies and yet we all just lay there and wait for it to happen. Actors playing their parts.

A nurse comes in to say that they are ready. You start on your final journey to the operating room. Again, you realize this is a journey that you have to take alone. No matter that family and friends wait just a short distance away, you alone must face what is ahead. A journey for but one.

The operating crew is very cheerful. Each one introduces himself to me. They are extremely efficient and in a few moments I have been positioned on the operating table. As the room is quite cold, a warm blanket is placed from my waist down. It feels wonderful and somehow very reassuring. An oxygen mask is placed over my nose and mouth and my various IV's are connected. Someone says that Dr. Gomes is on the way down and I hear the anesthesiologist say, "I'm going to put him under now." Then nothing. No sensations, no thoughts, no dreams. Only a black void. Nothing.

Finally Dr. Gomes strode in and reported that he had done seven resections of the lower lobe, more than he had expected. Two of the tumors were so small he could feel but not see them. Such sensitivity comes from much experience. Warmth and compassion shone from his eyes, and I had complete faith in his skill as a surgeon. Again, hugs all around and the wait until I could join Mark in his room.

This operation was much longer and more complicated than the first one. In order to operate on the lung, his ribs were cracked and spread apart. Mark was still very groggy when the nurse wheeled him into his room. I immediately began Reiki healing on him as music from my subliminal healing tape filled the room. Much later when I left, I asked the nurse to turn the tape over whenever she was in his room. The next day I learned she had done this every thirty minutes during the night. Positive healing affirmations had bathed Mark's subconscious all night long.

During the drive back to the boat I encountered a tremendous thunderstorm. Fierce lightning streaked the sky and was almost instantaneously followed by deafening thunder. The rain fell so heavily I could only occasionally see the white line leading down the middle and into total darkness. Like the rain, my tears poured down in heavy torrents as I comprehended the reality of Mark's cancer. With each thunderclap I cried louder—sharing my passion with nature's. The storm ebbed, as did my tears. In the sky, silver linings glistened around the edges of soft pink cumulus clouds. I fell into deep awe of nature's power and beauty and its symbolic promise of hope and comfort, and I wept again.

After Mark's lung operation, it truly sank in—the cancer might still be lurking elsewhere in his body. This time we had no assurance that the doctors had gotten it all. After Mark's kidney was removed, we had gone home fat, dumb, and happy believing—hoping against hope—he was cured for good. Who knows? Maybe, given the power of positive thinking, forgetting the cancer was the best thing we could have done. Or were we in denial? Could it be that denial kept us from starting some sort of a prevention program? During those two years of reprieve, we tried to keep cancer out of sight and out of mind. Certainly the doctors offered no suggestions for how to prevent the cancer from recurring. Perhaps they had no insights either.

According to death and dying expert Elisabeth Kübler-Ross, denial is the first stage of the death and dying process. Several years earlier, when I started my search for the meaning of life, I was inexplicably drawn to read everything I could find on death and dying. Mark and the girls thought I was a bit ghoulish as I brought home yet another armload of books on the topic. Then one day my sister Mayva called: another sister, Phyllis, had bone marrow cancer. I was stunned. Phyllis, who called me her little twin, was too young and vibrant to be dying. Drawing on the wisdom from my research on death helped me through this period. It also enabled me to discuss and pass books on to members of the family, especially her two daughters. We discussed spiritual healing and I introduced them to Spiritual Frontiers Fellowship, a source of local support.

A poignant moment, etched in my memory forever, happened when I visited Phyllis in the Minnesota hospital. She was to be allowed to go home for one day between treatments. Phyllis wanted to sit in the sunshine on her back deck, something she dearly loved to do. But the next morning it rained. Disappointed for her, I said, "Oh, Phyllis, I'm so sorry it's not a nice day." She smiled gently and said, "Joan, *every* day is a nice day." Phyllis died, just one year after diagnosis.

Now, as Mark slowly recovered, I recalled the five stages of dying: denial, anger, bargaining, depression, and acceptance. But reading about death and dying and facing it with my dear husband were two very different things.

During his hospital stay we began learning everything we could about renal cell carcinoma. The facts were not encouraging. Mark was in stage four, the final stage, with the poorest prognosis. We learned that distant metastasis from renal cell carcinoma are most commonly found in the lungs, bones, and liver. Okay, we knew cancer had spread to his lungs. Had it also spread to the bones and liver?

An oncologist came into his room late one evening. He explained to Mark there was no known cure for his type of cancer nor any methods of treatment that were really very effective. They could put Mark on a chemotherapy program just to be doing something, but that made no sense. Chemotherapy is basically a process of poisoning the whole body in the hopes that the normal cells will out survive the cancer cells. There had to be a better way. He didn't say how much time Mark could expect to live nor did Mark ask. The doctor suggested that Mark's best bet was to try to get into an experimental cancer program at the National Institute of Health (NIH) in Bethesda. This was not reassuring to Mark as several years earlier he had tried unsuccessfully to help get his boss into NIH. Seeing his boss, whom Mark loved like a father, fight a losing battle with cancer had been devastating. Paul's death left a great sadness in Mark's life. Since Mark did not discuss his feelings, I never realized how much until later.

That night, alone in his dark room, in pain from the incisions, uncomfortable from the tubes running down his throat and sticking out of his side to drain the lung, Mark pondered his future. "I didn't sleep well," he told me later.

Chapter Five

Rallying Resources for an Uncharted Journey

Since traditional Western medicine offered us little hope, we felt forced to find our own path. I felt that if Mark had any chance to survive, it was through strengthening and mobilizing his own immune system to kill off the cancer cells. Alternative medicine, healthy foods, biofeedback, meditation, visualization, and positive thinking seemed to be our only choice. On my spiritual search, I studied *A Course in Miracles*. The course states there is no order of difficulty in miracles. One is not "harder" or "bigger" than another. I decided to expect one.

Even before Mark left the hospital, I began to rally resources and people who might be able to help him. Since Mark was the practical, down-to-earth type, I was afraid he would discount much of what I'd say as just more of my "weird" ideas.

When Stan and Shirley visited Mark at the hospital, I explained in private I wanted them to visit us the following week. I suggested Stan talk to Mark about the power of the mind and its ability to activate the immune system. I hoped Mark would accept these ideas if he heard them from Stan, a physician.

I discussed with Mark how important it was to feed the brain positive healing messages. In the hospital, Mark asked me to read aloud to him from a novel about the Vietnam War. As I read aloud about the killing, the hate, and the child prostitution, I got such a visceral reaction I had to put it down. I tried to explain. If my healthy body reacted negatively to these images, how would they impact his vulnerable immune system? "How can healing take place in your body, if your mind is thinking about hate and killing? Garbage in, garbage out." Mark didn't say anything, but he began to read more positive books, including some I suggested.

Many of these books focused on the person's attitude, especially on forgiveness and on releasing fear and anger. They stress that attitudinal healing precedes physical healing. Although I believe attitude does play an important role in healing, I felt some of the authors gave simple, pat answers. Many people who are told they create their illness feel tremendous guilt. I didn't want Mark to feel that way.

It is such a puzzle—a confusing mind-body-soul puzzle: if we do create our own illness, we do so unconsciously. As a result, all we can do is consciously choose how we react to that illness. After some hesitation, I made all my books available; Mark could decide if he wanted to read them or not. I also sent away for information on Commonweal, a program designed to objectively study alternative and adjunctive cancer therapies.

Teresa wanted to help too and had sent Mark *A Gift of Healing*, excerpts from *A Course in Miracles*. It tells how our physical health reflects our desires and defenses, fantasies and fears, and that the first step toward being healed is to truly desire it. No miracle can be given you unless you want it.

As we collected resources, talked to people and went to healing services, Mark struggled to sort all this new information out in his own mind.

21 June 1990

Attended a healing service in Baltimore with Joan and Kristen. We arrived late and were just in time for the healing portion of the service. I didn't really have time to get mentally prepared and relaxed for the laying on of hands and even though I felt peaceful, I really didn't experience any other feeling during the process—i.e., no real awareness of a great healing presence. Maybe I am looking for some type of dramatic evidence that will clearly demonstrate to me and those around me that I have been healed in an instant, a blinding miracle that will allow me to walk out a whole, clean person. This obviously didn't happen.

During the entire day I felt quite down and confused over what is actually taking place within my body and what my actual role in this whole process should be. The question of whether I am now trying to do things I normally wouldn't do, just to try and cure this illness, keeps coming up. Do I really believe that I have the power to receive divine healing or is this just some desperate act on my part to try and reverse a process that is meant to be? Sometimes I feel I have already received this healing and other times I don't. A confusing pattern of thoughts that leave one feeling quite empty. In brief, I don't feel as optimistic over the eventual outcome of this problem as I have in the past and perhaps I am just questioning too much God's willingness to heal me.

I know I should let it all go and just trust but this is much easier said than done. Trying to change the "old me" is not an easy task. What I really need now is another flood of assurance that I have received in the past that everything is going to be okay but this has not been forthcoming. Perhaps that's something that is not given on a recurring basis, but is something that one receives but once, and from that point on, one must rely on trusting that it has been received.

Other thoughts of the day revolve around questioning whether I really want to be healed and if this is the reason for doubting whether healing has been received. Am I the actual fly in my own ointment and if so, why? All this is based on my recent reading which states that the choice of whether to be well or ill, to live or to die, is really up to me. If this is so, why do I keep questioning the feeling I once had that everything is going to be okay unless I really do not want this to be so. Why would anyone consciously make such a choice? I really don't have an honest answer. (Written at 0230 on 22 June)

Do you want healing or do you want death? Why would anyone question such a choice? And yet, if the choice is really mine to make, why do I keep questioning the feeling I once had that everything is going to be fine and my cancer is never going to show up again unless I myself do not want this to happen? Why all this doubt and how do you really make it go away? I hope answers will be forthcoming. (Written after reading from _A Gift of Healing_ at 0400 same date)

22 June 1990

To live or die. Doesn't seem like it would be hard to choose which to do but today has been full of periods of doubt as to which I really want. If, as _A Gift of Healing_ states, the choice of which road to follow is really up to each individual, why then do I feel so strongly sometimes that this decision has already been made for me and I have only to accept this fact and let go of life? Letting go seems so easy to do at this point that I have to wonder if this is something my own mind has come up with or whether it is being generated from a much higher source. Is this really my time to go?

This morning we helped a friend bring his boat back from the West River. As I drove it down the Bay on what had to be one of the truly most gorgeous days of the year, I kept asking myself whether anyone would consciously choose to depart from such a beautiful world if the choice was actually up to them. I really don't have an answer at this time and must keep searching. Perhaps the word, "must," does not accurately describe how I feel at this point of time and would better be replaced by the word, "should," but accepting this seems to be a form of letting go so I have to try and generate new enthusiasm for the search.

Also this morning as we came down the Bay I watched Kristen and realized just how much I love her, as well as Joan and Teresa, and I asked myself how could anyone choose to leave them if any other choice was available. The best I could come up with was, "I really don't know." This again made me wonder if the choice is really up to me or whether I am trying to fight a process that is preordained. Why shouldn't this be my time?

I suppose that to each individual there is never a perfect time to go so why shouldn't this be mine when the acceptance of death seems so easy and while the acceptance of life seems so questionable? Hopefully some answers will be forthcoming soon.

23 June 1990

For the first time the early morning hours (0230) brought worries about how this entire process is going to affect us financially. These were worries that I have, up to now, been able to keep from thinking about, but this morning they would not easily be dismissed even though I was conscious of their negative impact on my overall well being. Even Joan's assurances that "Everything will work out just fine" didn't seem to have the normal reassuring effect on me. I know that I will have to put such worries behind me if I am to have any chance for the healing process to work. Again, if I know all this, why is it now next to impossible to do? Up to now all I have had to do when such thoughts came up was to mentally say that I can't be bothered by such things and that I am turning them over to God. For the first time since I entered the hospital, this process did not work and it left me feeling that I am back to square one again on just trusting fully in God's willingness to handle such things. I hope this was just a momentary relapse for if it is not, I am certainly not making any progress in this entire process.

An afternoon visit and several hours of conversation with Stan, Shirley and Joan did a lot to change my whole outlook on my present situation. Stan told of his gradual conversion from strictly a doctor's trained viewpoint of "we can fix anything" to one of realizing that the greatest healing source of all is contained within each and everyone of us—our immune system.

His belief that what is really required is for me to work on methods to trigger this system into wiping out any remaining cancer cells and not to rely only on doctors to cure my illness. He believes that the two should work together but that the stronger of the two is certainly my own immune system.

We had further discussions regarding changing of thought patterns (or pathways) and that it is not done overnight. Joan's comments on this were also very helpful. All in all, I feel that I made a tremendous amount of progress on refocusing my attention away from why I have my current illness and is it something I actually wanted, to "how do I cure it?" The feeling is wonderful and I only hope it lasts. Questioning this is probably one of the old thought patterns I will have to break. Something good and wonderful was given me, so just use it!

24 June, 1990

Had an excellent night's sleep and awoke with the same good feeling I acquired yesterday. After reading more from *A Gift of Healing*, many of the old doubts and questions started coming back so perhaps the message in this book is not exactly what I need at this time. By mid-morning the good feeling had returned, though somewhat tempered by watching Kristen getting ready to leave.

The first thoughts of how can I use my current experiences to help others are starting to form, but I realize that I have a long way to go before I really have a good grasp on the entire picture.

The rest of the day was fine. It was good to visit with Bonnie and Rodney who came out about noon and brought a wonderful assortment of food. Unlike the conversations of the previous day, we just talked about everyday things. No spiritual gain but no loss either.

Teresa's arrival from Florida was the highlight of the day and provided a great lift.

In the summer of 1990, Teresa and Kristen both quit their jobs in Florida to move back to Virginia, where they shared an apartment in Alexandria. Teresa accepted a position with a former employer. Kristen entered graduate school. Although Mark was delighted to have them nearby, he hoped their decision to move wasn't because of him. He worried about the effect his illness might have on them.

Mark let me read his journal, and it formed the basis for some of our best discussions. After reading his first entries, including his reaction to _A Gift of Healing_, I thought Teresa also needed to know the struggle going on within her dad. Mark said she could read his journal too. Teresa left a very touching letter tucked in his journal. Writing seemed to make some communication easier.

Dear Dad,

Mom said it was okay to read through your journal to get a handle on how you are feeling. The changing of patterns of a lifetime is never an easy process, and I admire you more than you know for your willingness to embrace new experiences and thought patterns. What I have learned through my spiritual journey is to take those things that "feel right" and discard the rest. They may not be "bad," but you just might not be ready for them. So if _Gift of Healing_ is bothering you, put it aside! I have found many things that made sense the second or third time I picked them up and still many more that still don't feel right.

I shared with mom that Bapa [Mark's father] came into my workroom during a healing meditation for you. He looked as he did when I was 10. He patted my cheek and said, "Dearest little Teresa, everything will be all right." But I got the definite feeling that it was going to require work on all our parts.

I don't know why it is so much easier to have negative thoughts rather than positive ones—but it is. I guess the question might be, "if" (a big if!) you are not going to beat the cancer, would you rather spend your remaining time consumed by negative thoughts or positive actions? As to the purpose behind why something like this happens, who knows? But I do see a lot of good manifesting from this "negative" experience.

You have reminded a lot of people just what is important in life. Material possessions and individual achievement can never be a substitute for the love of family and friends. The number of cards and calls indicate just how many lives you have touched, and a lot of us are taking a closer look at how we live!

Keep positive and know that you can never underestimate the power of the circle of love that surrounds you. I love you.

Teresa

P.S. I know how hard this time is for you (I can sympathize, not empathize). I hope you can appreciate how taxing it is for Mom. Sometimes it is harder to watch someone you love go through difficult times. She needs support also.

P.P.S. Your search is like one of your crossword puzzles: you have an immediate answer to some of the questions. Some you think you know, until the words around your answer make you change that answer. And some words are only clear after all of the other answers have been supplied!

At the same time as Teresa had felt her Bapa's presence, Mark and I also were aware of him. One morning I had my hand on Mark's forehead as we meditated and I felt a heavy hand on top of mine. Somehow I knew that it was Mark's dad's hand. I didn't say anything. At that moment Mark said, "Dad appeared in my dream last night. He was so real." The next day, too, as we meditated Mark said his dad floated into his imagery. I felt thankful he was helping us from Spirit.

Teresa had also left a letter for me.

Dear Mom,

You have kindled the light of spirituality in so many people—and I for one will be forever thankful for you. I know this situation is difficult for you, but you have to remember that you can't fix everything. This is Dad's fight, and no matter how bad you want to, you can't take responsibility for his life. I know that is hard for you to accept (really, deep down accept, because I think you do accept it intellectually). You want to fix the bad things in the lives of those you love—and certainly you can help. But ultimately we must sit on the sidelines, an active but still separate audience.

Take care of yourself and your needs (the humor workshop you had been looking forward to and canceled!) Otherwise you won't be much help to anyone. This is a true test of everything you have said you believe and it is a great opportunity to practice all you have preached—but remember, even Jesus had his low moments of doubt and depression (in the garden of Gethsemane!), so don't discount those emotions or cover them up. If Jesus felt them, then I guess you can too! I love you.

Teresa

Chapter Six

Energy, Attitude, and Food

Mark did not resonate with *A Course in Miracles* and we agreed to put it aside. He used techniques to quiet his mind and develop healing visualizations and agreed to my doing Reiki healing with him every day. Once a week, Jean and Merrill joined me in giving Mark Reiki. They volunteer at the Institute for Attitudinal Studies, a nonprofit educational and spiritual organization dedicated to personal growth and being of service. As a service, the Institute offers support groups and individual facilitation for those with life-threatening illnesses. Jean and Merrill used these facilitation skills when we'd discuss healing principles after each Reiki session. Mark needed to hear these concepts from someone besides me. Mark would say things to them he hadn't expressed to me. This clarified his point of view for me. The fact that Merrill is a retired nuclear engineer and Jean a retired head nurse gave them credibility in Mark's eyes.

Jean gave me *Recalled by Life* by Tony Satellario, a doctor given a few months to live who reversed his cancer by going on the macrobiotic diet. I'd never considered or looked at diet changes. Mark loved to eat—"lived to eat" perhaps expresses it better. When we lived and traveled abroad, Mark always remembered where and what we ate. We even planned travel agendas so as to return to his favorite restaurants.

Because food was so important to Mark, I had become an excellent cook—and "excellent" meant lots of rich foods like butter, cream, meats, and sweets. I agreed with the central concept of Satellario's book that foods contribute to health or to disease. It makes sense that consistently eating the wrong foods adds stress to the body and organs. Hadn't we already had a warning several years ago, just before his fiftieth birthday? Then, after Mark drank many cups of eggnog made with heavy cream, I ended up rushing him to the hospital where he subsequently had his gall bladder removed. I also remember the surgeon saying after he had removed it that it was good, because now Mark could eat anything he wanted. We never thought to ask why his gall bladder went bad. Just life and bad luck. No one told us and we didn't ask. But when you think about it, nature is frugal. We don't come with spare parts. Everything has a purpose. So what organ takes over the gall bladder's job if it is removed? Now I seriously began to question the effect food has on the body.

I believe life is a balance of physical, mental, emotional, and spiritual components. When any one of those areas gets out of balance or is unduly stressed, the body becomes more vulnerable to illness. Scientists say cancer cells appear in our bodies all the time. Most of the time, we simply discard them. Cancer cells are also supposedly weak, confused adolescent cells that never grow up. Thus they don't mature, die, and leave the body as normal cells do. What triggers their building up and being able to take over? Stress of all kinds can weaken the immune system and allow this to happen.

So many factors have an impact on the physical body: toxins and chemicals in our food, air, and water; electromagnetic fields. We can't do anything about many of these things—after all, we have to continue to breathe as we inch through the urban gridlock. But we can choose what we eat and drink. We can give the immune system a decent chance to do what it is so brilliantly designed to do. But macrobiotics? We're talking major change of diet. I never dreamed that Mark would be willing to do it. Mark used to point to his father, who ate nearly a stick of butter a day and lived to be over 103 years old, even remarrying at age 92. Mark's cholesterol was a low 130, so we didn't think eating that way was a problem.

I decided just to pass the book on to Mark and wait for his reaction.

25 June 1990

Slept quite well and upon awakening about 0230 I experimented with ways to stop unwanted thought patterns. Found that when unwanted thoughts started, i.e., potential financial problems, if I projected these thoughts on a blackboard I could take an eraser and wipe them out. This technique seemed to work well. I will have to be positive in everything that I do or think as a very important part of the cleansing process. Not healing since I am not ill, but rather cleansing, since I have a few potentially bad cells to get rid of.

Worked hard on various techniques for improving my visualization for ridding my body of unwanted cells. I found that having the good white cells, (interns in white coats) collect any questionable and potentially dangerous bad cells and simply put them in a special box seemed to work quite well. This seems to be more of a recognition on my part that I am totally free of cancer at this time and only have to make sure that nothing is now allowed to turn into it. Having white cells make a complete and frequent body search to catch any cells in the process of turning bad seems like a good way to go.

Had a good session with Merrill and Jean and again felt vibration in my right leg from Joan's hands and on my left side from either Merrill or Jean. The conversation with them afterwards was rewarding and I left feeling very confident that I am really starting to be in control.

Afternoon mail contained a medical review which painted a very dim picture on my type of cancer. Basically no type of effective treatment and statistics on chances to survive for three to five years not good. I've already survived two of those years. Only five percent make it to five years.

After an initial feeling of a great let down, I was able to regain a positive attitude by looking at it as a greater challenge to beat the odds or statistics. As a result, my interns in white coats redoubled their efforts in bad cell control and it was easy to open up doors to different parts of my body and actually visualize them going about their tasks.

In the early evening I started to read *Recalled by Life* by Anthony Sattiliaro, M.D. Unfortunately I only got through the first forty-one pages, where he describes the personal devastation he felt on learning he had cancer and the pain and suffering of the following operations. Knowing how he felt, I could actually go through the entire process with him and it left me feeling completely down and drained.

Many researchers correlate mental imagery and physical health. Physicians like Benson, Siegel, and Simonton, teach their patients to use visualization as a tool for strengthening their immune systems. I was happy that Mark chose a visualization that was aggressive but without malice or hate.

I remembered the story of an Amish man who did not respond well until he changed his visualization from one of killer white cells attacking cancer cells to a visualization of white cells lovingly carrying the cancer cells and depositing them outside the body. He was then true to his core belief in nonviolence and his health began to improve.

Mark was a history buff and loved to read about all the wars and military interventions. I guess I expected his imagery to be full of bombs bursting in air and killing fields. For me, hate in any form is harmful even if directed at your cancer cells. But a visualization has to be personal, no one else can choose it.

26 June 1990

Awoke about 0300 in a heavy sweat and felt very down. Tried to visualize my intern network at work internally but nothing materialized. Felt that the whole network had gone to sleep or had been destroyed and I was left with a very empty and despondent feeling. Further mental review convinced me of several things:

1. It would be very, very easy to give up.

2. My present level of conviction and confidence that I am in charge and can direct the process to a successful conclusion is not very strong or lasting. Note: THE "I" REFERS NOT ONLY TO ME BUT ALSO TO THE DIVINE AND OTHER POWERS that hopefully are guiding and controlling my actions.

3. Never end your reading or conversation on a negative note. My whole belief structure is too fragile at this point in time to withstand it!

I trust I can regain and expand lost confidence today. I want to get back that feeling that my illness has a real divine meaning and purpose rather than being just a means to remove me from this earth.

Further readings in *Recalled by Life* took me through the sections where the author is introduced to macrobiotic cooking and accepts and follows it. I have no problem in accepting the idea that a changed diet can totally alter your health and well being.

For years I have felt that two major changes over the past twenty-five and thirty years have had a tremendously negative impact on our health as evidenced by our alarming increase in the incidents of cancer and heart disease. These changes are the increased levels of pollution in the atmosphere and our changing eating habits (fast-fooditis). My intake of atmospheric pollution is almost impossible to control but I can control my diet and have tried to modify it over the past few years as I felt necessary.

The general gauge has been my physical checkups and as long as my blood pressure and tests have been normal (or outstanding!) I have felt that my diet has been okay. Now with two outbreaks of cancer, for which medical science can not offer any causal reasons, I really believe that my diet certainly has to be considered as a prime suspect.

Given the fact that it is also something I can control, I want to explore macrobiotic cooking much more deeply. It also means that I can take additional immediate action to rid my body of any remaining cancer cells and not just wait for them to settle and grow into tumors large enough to be detected so that the doctors might be able to treat them. Hopefully the doctors will never have to get into the act! Perhaps something as simple as certain foods is the triggering mechanism for my cancer and if so, I intend to find out and do something about it.

27 June 1990

Had a good night's sleep and about 0200 awoke after having a dream where an SST type aircraft was diving almost straight down toward a spot very close to where I was standing with a group of unknown people in a city I could not identify. As it came closer to the ground its angle of dive grew steeper until it became obvious that the plane was going to crash. As it disappeared behind the tree and roof line, we waited to see a giant ball of flame and smoke. But nothing happened. We stood there waiting until word filtered back that somehow the plane had stopped short of hitting the ground and was now hovering so the passengers could escape. In thinking about this, it was easy to see me as being that aircraft in a final dive toward destruction who somehow was given the chance to pull out short of total destruction. Even the hovering part seemed to say that I am not totally safe yet and that there are things I must do to be sure that this destruction does not occur.

With this dream coming right on the heels of the diet revelation I received yesterday, there is no doubt in my mind that completely changing my eating patterns and habits is what is needed if I am to free myself of cancer. Eating is certainly one of the constant factors throughout this entire process and I now feel that it may be the key to the successful eradication of my cancer problem. Joan's quote that she uses in workshops, "If you keep on doing what you are doing, you're going to keep on getting what you're getting," seems very appropriate. I don't want any more cancer.

This is not to say that other things such as stress and tension have not also contributed to my problem but I believe that a proper diet may go a long ways toward helping me reduce these as well. I also believe that a changed diet will not be the sole factor in eliminating my cancer and that I will have to keep working and growing in other areas as well. It is, however, the one thing that has been given me (and I really mean given) where I can become "hands on involved" and not have to just rely on what others are doing for me, be this either in the field of medicine or the area of spiritual healing. I firmly believe that God has given me what I need at this time and I give my heartfelt thanks to Him and the people through whom all this is coming.

My morning appointment with Dr. Gomes went well. Had a chest X-ray, which showed no problems. The healing process has been excellent. Had a brief conversation with him regarding the fact that the first oncologist I talked to seemed very vague about the whole approach to treating my cancer and indicated that until this disease strikes again, they will just sit back and wait.

Dr. Gomes said that sometimes people who are unsure of themselves tend to come across in a somewhat unclear manner. He further stated that under the above approach he should have left some of the cancer nodules in place so the oncologists could have started their treatment and that this made no sense whatever. He went on to state that he thought Dr. Anders would be much more positive in his approach and seemed to suggest I hold off further judgment until I meet with him.

I went on to say that I couldn't, under any circumstances, just sit back and wait for cancer to strike again but had to go on a program to prevent its reoccurrence. I further stated my belief that strengthening my own immune system was the best source for prevention and that I had to find a way to make it kick in and take over. Dr. Gomes agreed and said that he could, within limits, surgically remove the infected parts should cancer strike again, but that the answer was to avoid the necessity of surgery. Prevention instead of removal.

At the end Dr. Gomes pulled up info on my brain scan and said that everything is normal. A relief to me but a much larger relief to Joan who evidently had, because of my history of headaches, been very worried over what the brain scan might show.

The rest of the day was upbeat and went smoothly. Almost like a reprieve has been issued—the cancer is gone and all we have to do now is keep it from coming back.

Mark had a bone and brain scan to see if cancer had metastasized anywhere else. These tests were necessary if we were going to try to get him into the NIH experimental program. When a friend visited Mark in the hospital, she told us she'd just watched a television special about how Lee Remick had received the treatment for renal cancer at NIH and was doing well. It was so encouraging to hear success stories—and, conversely, a big disappointment when we learned a year later that Lee Remick had died.

28 June 1990

During the night I awoke several times and started wondering whether I am underestimating the difficulty of the battle I face and am counting on an apparently simple and easy fix like changing my eating habits to work a miracle that is eluding the best efforts of medical science. Am I just grasping at straws or is the answer so simple that the medical experts can't accept it? Surely if diet can be linked to cancer, diet change should also be able to help cure it. Makes logical sense but its absolute simplicity seems to argue against it. Well, I'm part of the experiment now so let's see where it leads me.

Finished reading *Recalled by Life* and it is amazing to recognize the parallels between the author's feelings and questions and my own. Of special significance is the sameness in questioning what our new purpose in life is meant to be. At first I wondered why it had taken the author almost two years of cancer to face this most important question while I am really facing it only three weeks after surgery. It finally dawned on me that the first bout with cancer left me a basically unchanged person who "took off a weekend to have cancer" and then resumed a normal life. I have actually been involved in this process for almost two years, yet only the second cancer attack got my attention and made me realize that if I want to continue living (and I do) I must make a dramatic change in my lifestyle in order to make this possible.

Chapter Seven

Visualizations Meditations, and Humor

29 June 1990

Spent a restless night with a lot of time being spent dealing with various doubts. Doubts as to whether I will really survive this or whether I am just generating false hopes. Doubts about our finances since the market for the boat, or for our lots, doesn't seem to exist. Doubts about my physical condition being sound enough to allow me to generate additional revenues and on and on.

I didn't seem able to just shut my thought patterns off, for when they hit, they were already in a complete package and could be seen in their entirety in an instant, i.e., they were fully conceived and required no further development and were totally comprehended the instant they entered my mind. This was a different process for me and the only good aspect was that the doubts contained in these thoughts didn't produce the real gut-wrenching feeling that they have in the past. Perhaps this means I am making progress. The possibility that all the above was due to concern I may have over my bone scan today also comes to mind but since I really believe that the scan will turn out fine, I can't know for sure.

Once during the night I felt very close to Dad. This feeling lasted but for an instant and I can't really say that I actually felt his presence but I also can't say for sure that I didn't either. It all happened so fast that I am not certain as to exactly what took place but I feel quite certain that something certainly did.

At 1000 we were at the hospital for my bone scan procedure. The technician injecting the radioactive dye had trouble hitting a vein and took two tries. Her first miss of the week—spoiled her perfect record.

During the three-hour wait for the dye to spread throughout my body, we drove over to pick up books on macrobiotics that our friend had left at her school. Per her usual helpful way, she had left a shopping bag (properly addressed) full of material with a detailed outline with suggestions on where to start reading.

When Mark agreed to go on the macrobiotic diet, I felt eager to begin. This was something tangible I could do to help. Once we decided, people and resources began flooding in to us. I discovered a friend of mine was macrobiotic and I didn't even know it. I just knew she had the energy of ten people, never put on an extra pound, and had not aged in the twenty-some years I'd known her—in fact, she looked younger! Along with the shopping bag full of books Mark spoke of in his journal, she introduced us to the local macrobiotic community, which met for potluck dinners, lectures, and cooking lessons.

Back at the hospital we spent about an hour and a half in the cafeteria reading and having lunch. The more I read, the more I am realizing just how important a changed diet, along with changes in thought patterns and general lifestyle will be in eliminating my cancer. It made sense that if my misuse of these factors caused cancer in the first place (and I am now certain that it did), then the only way to eliminate it is to change the way I have been doing things.

The bone scan itself took about forty minutes and the first thing I noticed as the image of my upper internal structure was flashed on the viewing monitor were several flickering red spots. My immediate reaction was, "Oh no, my cancer has spread to my bones." I asked the technician conducting the test about it and she said that the red spots indicated pooling of the dye but did not necessarily indicate any problem as some pooling in certain areas was normal and that only the doctors could tell if a problem existed. Readouts won't be available until Thursday's session with Dr. Anders.

I wanted Mark to meditate because it is the single most important thing I do for myself that helps me stay centered and peaceful. At the same time, I knew my way is a "feeling" approach, and Mark's way was a "thinking" approach. Mark would need to receive instructions from a man on how best to meditate. With this in mind, I called Jim, a friend of mine who is a retired Ph.D. anthropologist. He and his wife practice meditation and eat a macrobiotic diet. When Mark and I visited them, she took me out to the kitchen to teach me how to make *gomasio*, a sesame seed and sea salt condiment, while he talked to Mark about meditation and guided him in a practice session. When Mark began to meditate with me daily, I was happy as I felt we connected on a heart level for some greater purpose.

30 June 1990

Slept extremely well during the night and even when I awoke I didn't have any "worry" thought patterns and went right back to sleep. Could, perhaps, skipping a sweet desert in the evening have resulted in no sugar overload in my system? Sugar overload tends to cause and support tension and stress (per macrobiotics philosophy). Perhaps the changes I am already making in my eating habits are having an affect on certain of my systems. I certainly hope so.

Just before getting out of bed, I started my morning visualization of my white coated interns doing their clean-up routines of my internal systems. For some reason I did not feel that visualizing them with their normal brooms and dustpans was sufficient and so I gave them vacuum cleaners. At first this seemed to work well but after awhile this also seemed inadequate so I replaced them with interns with white coveralls and high rubber boots who were using high pressure water hoses and long handled brushes to really clean out even the most hidden places. This really seemed to be doing the job and as I was guiding them down through my body, Joan turned to me and said that during the night she had received a very clear message that it was most important that I continue with a very aggressive visualization program and that I do this five or six times a day. Coincidence? I think not!

Met with Jim in the afternoon and had a very nice session. Covered various aspects of how to successfully deal with and cure my cancer problem. It all made good sense and most of it I am already doing. He stressed the importance of exercise and I will have to start on a much more vigorous program, maybe even the disliked jogging. He also stressed the importance of visualization.

Had a lesson in meditation and that seemed to go well. Actually found myself twice returning to consciousness from some deeper level though I have no idea how long I was in that state.

Before we started the diet, we had dinner with our friends, Milde and Jim. We called it "our last supper." They served a mixed grill with lots of different meats and sweet desserts, and we indulged ourselves.

Their sons listened intently as the discussion focused on cancer and how we were planning to cope. Milde always relates some outrageous story, and we always laugh a lot when with her. I mentioned how important we thought humor was, and like Norman Cousins in *Anatomy of Illness*, we checked out funny books and videos. A friend from Michigan had just sent Mark a sports bloopers video. The youngest son listened with thoughtful concern showing in his big beautiful eyes, and he quietly left the room. He returned to stand silently in front of me with his outstretched hand holding a video. It was *The Three Stooges*. He said we could keep it as long as we wanted. All the bashing, poking, and bopping on the head the Three Stooges do made us wince, and I couldn't imagine it made our immune systems happy. But we told him we loved it—it was his compassion that mattered.

Had dinner at Milde's where we met their friend who is also recovering from cancer (an agent orange victim) and after a heavy meal—meat, meat, meat, fish, chicken, rice, salad, and cream pies—we had a very good and helpful discussion on beating cancer. Since three of the nine of us have had cancer, we, as a group, represented the new national statistic that one out of every three Americans will contract cancer in their lifetime. Just your normal average group.

It was interesting to see how much alike their friend's and my approach are toward our disease. He had been given radiation treatments and then told, "That's all, folks." He couldn't accept this and so set off to research and develop his own preventative program. In addition to visualization and exercise and trying to reduce his stress levels, he decided that the vitamin approach was what he needed. I can't say that at this point in my 'enlightenment' I can agree with his choice as being right for me but will carefully go over the research info he promised to share with me. Hope it works well for him as he is just coming up on the critical two-year period. Pray his next CAT scan will show him to be totally cancer-free.

1 July 1990

Didn't have a very restful night and wonder if it was due to the heavy meal I ate. I felt wrong doing it as I could almost sense that I was giving my body something it really didn't need. I wonder if I am putting too much importance on this business of diet but somehow I don't feel that I am. Completely changing my eating habits is certainly no easy answer to my problem—a quick fix so to speak—so I feel my commitment to this change is something I am being directed to do and I accept this direction willingly.

Couldn't get my visualization going last night or again this morning. My scrubbers seemed to have deserted me. Tried four or five times to get them back on the job but to no avail. Funny how something that was so vividly clear and worked so well yesterday could be lost so quickly. Could this be the price of my heavy meal?

Did a lot of reading about macrobiotics during the day and am becoming totally convinced that a proper diet is a big part of licking my problem. Felt a bit down but this is probably to be expected following the elation experienced during most of the proceeding day.

Worked on my visualization many times but was unable to bring it back to its former levels of ease and clarity. Meditation worked well and saw a clear vision of Dad.

Filled out my history for Monday's session with macrobiotic counselor, Michael Rossoff, and had problems in including the requested snake and dragon in the drawing I had to include. They didn't seem to fit in with the rest of the overall scene. Walked over three miles.

2 July 1990

Slept better last night and even though I had trouble getting to sleep initially, I was able to go back to sleep quickly on those occasions when I awoke. Worked on visualization every time I awoke but still not doing well. Perhaps I was too smug over my earlier successes.

Toward morning I changed my focus and started developing a scene where my immune system is seen as being a small factory inside my body and I can sit down at a control panel, turn a red-handled valve to increase white cell output and by controlling another dial instrument, direct them to different parts of my body where they absorb any bad black cells they find.

The thought just struck me that I lost my previous strong visual image after a friend told me that I had to see myself more involved in the actual cleansing process. When I tried to picture myself in this role, the entire vision left me. Could it be that what I was led to visualize was right for me just the way it was and that it was a mistake to change it to be what others thought it should be? I will try to bring it back in its original form and see what happens.

Had my first macrobiotics session with Michael Rossoff at 1130 and everything went very well. Had no problems in accepting what he had to say on the entire concept of how important a proper diet is to the well-being of our health and how different types of food react on our bodies. Of special interest was his statement that macrobiotics does not require that we embrace any new philosophy other than recognizing that there is a better, more natural way to eat and that by so doing, we can help change many aspects of our lives.

He went on to say that diet is only one element in our lives and that we must also work on reducing other negatives that affect us such as stress and worry but that a proper diet will help us in this regards also. He felt that such things as visualization, deeper spiritual development, and proper medical treatment are also important elements in any healing process and that they are not opposed to one another but parts of a whole picture.

Our afternoon Reiki session with Jean and Merrill went well and again I seemed to be just very relaxed and lost all sense of time. A discussion followed regarding visualization and both of them agreed that I must develop what seems right to me and not rely on what others think is needed. Makes sense to me.

Our first visit to a natural food store followed and we spent one and a half hours wandering around in a new world, trying to find the locations of all the unfamiliar food products we now require. Clerks were most helpful and we departed with a whole lot of stuff.

Joan cooked us our first macrobiotic dinner of fried noodles with onions, ginger and sesame oil, miso soup with tofu, and freshly sliced daikon with ume plum vinegar as a side dish. Everything tasted good and I left the table feeling very satisfied. Off to a good start.

I didn't ease into macrobiotics gradually. Once we decided to take the plunge, I threw out everything that was not macrobiotic and planned menus, read cookbooks, shopped for organic foods, soaked beans overnight, and so on. If we were going to do it, I wanted to do it right.

Everything took so long to cook, and it heated up the galley on the boat where I only had a three burner stove. I worried about whether we would get the proper nutrients and whether Mark's body could tolerate the predicted weight loss. Still I tried to maintain an attitude of calm and peace as I prepared the food; cooking the food with love is part of the macrobiotic philosophy.

3 July 1990

Spent quite a restful night and though I woke up several times, had no trouble getting back to sleep. Used periods when awake to visualize my new method of increasing my immune system's output of healing cells and it continued to work well even though I sometimes would fall asleep in the middle of the process. The scar area became much more painful during the night and I hope it is only due to the position in which I had been sleeping.

In the morning, the area around my chest scar continued to get more painful especially in the front and back where the ribs ends join. (Per Dr. Gomes these two areas took most of the strain when my ribs were spread.) Also I became very tired after my morning walk and had to lie down and rest.

In the afternoon we went shopping for macrobiotics "support supplies" during which time I became so tired I had to rest in the car. Also the pain in my chest kept getting worse.

After eating our evening meal, my vitality seemed to come back but chest pains continued to get worse. During our walk, I actually had to hold my right front chest area to control the pain. After returning I found it difficult to even sit comfortably and by the time I retired, it was impossible to find a comfortable position. About 1130 Joan suggested using the hot water bottle and this finally allowed me enough relief so that I could go to sleep.

4 July 1990

Did not have a restful night and awoke about every hour and a half. Utilized these time periods to practice visualizations. By morning the chest pains had returned to almost normal levels so that was good news. Will check with Michael to see if any of this could be associated with my body's cleansing process due to dietary change. Seems too soon for such a response, but who knows?

In mentally reviewing what I have been going through the past several weeks and what affect it has had on me, I noted three very positive things.

1. I have not really been angry (except for one brief instance when I had to cut a walk short due to Poozie just wandering around and finally heading back to the boat on her own). Not even driving in heavy traffic has produced its normal responses and I tend to let things just happen without letting it have a negative impact on me.

2. I have worried less and less about what is going to happen in the future. Part of this may, of course, be due to the amount of time, effort, and concern that has gone into other areas but I don't think that this can fully explain the change. I certainly am not living totally in the "now" but do seem to be getting much better at it.

3. I have not had any headaches.

Chapter Eight

Black Thursday with Western Medicine

Mark and I made an appointment with an oncologist at Georgetown to review the results of the bone scan and discuss any next steps in treatment. We could have called for the results but decided to wait for a face-to-face discussion. If it was bad news, we didn't want to hear it over the phone. We'd know soon enough.

I took along a tape recorder to tape the discussion with the doctor's permission. When I'm nervous and upset, I often don't hear correctly, or Mark and I will hear different things, or we forget the details. I thought the tape would be helpful.

As we turned the corner to enter Vince Lombardi Cancer Center, I remembered last year when we walked by this wing Mark had looked down the corridor and said, "I hope I never have to go in there." Now here we were.

We passed by the children's center where they played and read as the IV units dripped chemicals into their small bodies. Mark shook his head and muttered, "That's got to be the worst."

We waited a long time before the doctor could see us—time in which to worry about everything! I felt low, fatigued from all the emotional strain as well as from the all-consuming effort to become macrobiotic and the rapid weight loss. While I was happy to lose my unnecessary pounds, it pained me to see the sharp angles of bones protruding from Mark's beautiful body. I thought about Mark's courage and willingness to try things that were foreign to him. I wanted to do more to help him. Maybe the best way I could help him was to continue to model positive healing behaviors. To maintain my own strength, I had to take time to center myself daily. When my own power wasn't enough, I had to turn it all over to a higher source of energy. This day was to be one of those times.

After two hours we were finally shown into the examining room. There we waited another half hour. Georgetown is a teaching hospital so everything takes longer, as interns need to be briefed and involved. When one is waiting to hear if cancer had metastasized to the bones or not, however, it seems barbaric to wait so long.

Dr. Anders (not his real name) finally entered briskly. In an intense and very businesslike manner, he immediately rattled off statistics of stage-four renal cell carcinoma and the lack of effective treatments. I pushed the record button on the tape recorder so I wouldn't miss anything. I didn't feel comfortable interrupting him to ask permission.

He continued in his blunt presentation, perhaps with the intent of being as honest and forthright as he could. Halfway through his comments, he noticed my tape recorder and abruptly asked me to turn it off, saying taping was unnecessary because he would explain everything and answer all our questions. I meekly did as I was told.

He didn't mention the bone scan until the end and only when we asked about it. He had not seen it but told us that the report said it was positive—cancer had spread to the bones—in the shoulder area and in the ribs. No, he didn't know to what degree. We were left not knowing much except that Mark's condition did not look good.

5 July 1990

Black Thursday. Met with two oncologists, Dr. Monty (not his real name), who was in training, and Dr. Anders. Anders turned out to be a very cold and seemingly uncaring individual who dealt in straight facts. Bottom line is that there is very little that can be done with renal cancer and success is measured in giving the patient a certain amount of relief and perhaps some extra time. The greatest chance for this happening is at NIH which he described as having a very physically tough and dangerous program. At best, they have been able to help approximately 17 percent of the 700 patients they have treated. There is no guarantee that I will be accepted into their program as I have to successfully pass a pulmonary breathing and a heart stress test.

Dr. Anders further stated that patients have died while undergoing NIH treatment but that in his opinion it offered the best hope and that I should undergo the tests and if I pass, talk to the NIH doctors to get more info on which to make a final decision. With that advice, "Dr. Friendly" ended the session after giving instructions to set the wheels in motion.

He forgot to mention that my bone scans came back positive though he had not himself seen them nor did he make any attempt to get a readout on the CAT Scan I had taken at 0700 that morning. All in all, a very unprofessional performance on the part of the doctors involved. Almost like saying that since they knew what the final outcome was going to be they really weren't too concerned about the details along the way. Just "another statistic in the making on which (not even who) we need not waste much of our valuable time." And, "On to those who stand a better chance of staying around longer, thus generating more revenues!"

Joan and I sat quietly in the examination room for a few minutes in a totally stunned condition. Not even tears would come. Plenty of time for that later. I had just heard my own death sentence pronounced and it

takes a bit of time to start really comprehending the
finality of what you have heard. I know and accept
that all of us must die sometime and saying this has
always been easy for me. But here and now I have
been told that my remaining time span on earth will
probably be measured in just months, for, per Anders,
we are dealing with a very nasty cancer. Not years
but months! But how can this be possible as I have so
many things that I still want to do? Then it hits that
such decisions may no longer be in our hands and it
leaves one with a very empty feeling. To say that we
were both devastated may not truly describe our feelings. Although I felt perfectly calm, I felt totally empty.
Just as if everything important in my life had been
removed in an instant and I was left with a complete
void that I would have to fill with something. But with
what? What is really important anymore?

We left in shock. There were no tears. We didn't talk.
We stopped at the health food store on the way home to
pick up a few things, but it was as if we were sleepwalking.
We wandered aimlessly around the store not knowing where
things were or what we needed—not really wanting any of
it.

We got back to the boat, turned on the air conditioner
to cool the muggy interior, and changed into shorts. Then
the dam burst. We both started to cry, me very loudly with
body-racking sobs and Mark with his mouth open and con-
torted, with no sound coming out, but his body heaving in
agony. I'd seen Mark with leaky eyes before, but I had never
seen him cry this way. We clung to each other.

I had never felt such grief; I knew I couldn't stand it
alone. With the first wave of emotion exhausted we lay
spent on the bed together. I had my hands on Mark's forehead and chest and told Spirit I needed help. I asked for a
sign we were not alone, that Spirit was with us. My hands
began to tingle and then the electricity increased steadily
until it soon felt as if I were hanging on to a high voltage

wire. The electrical current and vibration was extremely strong within my hands and up my arms even though Mark did not feel it. I thanked God for sending me a sign that He was with us now and for the strength to face whatever was ahead for us.

Mark focused his anger on Dr. Anders. Even if it was misplaced anger—anger at the messenger—it was healthy to express it. Bernie Siegel says it is a good sign if the patient rants and raves at the doctors. Such people are more likely to take control of their condition and not become passive victims. It is good to vent! I was not to know how long he held onto that anger until much later. To me, Dr. Ander's presentation of the findings displayed an unacceptable lack of sensitivity. While I didn't attribute it to greed or cold-heartedness, I realized we needed to shop around for a different oncologist.

I continued to do whatever I could to help Mark, praying and asking for guidance to find the right words, the right people, the right resources for all the ups and downs we were experiencing. Later that day I made calls to others on the macrobiotic diet who might have success stories I could share with Mark.

5 July 1990

The rest of the day passed almost in a semi-daze for although I was functioning, everything I did seemed to be mechanical and very unimportant. Had to force myself even to eat. After all, what difference would eating make in the long run? Back to being an actor in a play that someone else is directing. Just go through the expected motions and say the required lines, for after all, the play is going to close shortly!

Personally had a very bad period when I realized just how hard all this was impacting Joan and the girls. My real tears were not for myself but for them, for I felt that I was really letting them down or cheating them of something and that for the first time in my life I might have no control over the process. Funny how I never really felt like "poor me" but rather "poor them." Gee, perhaps I really do have some noble traits.

As the evening progressed, the feeling of total doubt began to be replaced by bits of hope. Perhaps if I am to demonstrate a true miracle taking place in my life, I have to first be put in a position where medical science has no hope. I feel I am now truly in such a position so now just trust and work to make it happen. Easy to say but so hard to do. At times like this I realize just how weak my faith and trust in God's good plan is and I must work to strengthen my faith.

The other thing that kept popping into my mind was that if macrobiotics is going to help, it certainly has an open field in which to do so. Here I don't mean just macrobiotics itself but rather our seeming to have been led to it at this point in time for I realize that this dietary concept is only one tool in an integrated healing plan that hopefully God has given and is continuing to reveal to me. No doubt in my mind that my cure would be something that medical science would find hard to refute and that if this is my true purpose in life, I would find it to be utterly fulfilling. What an opportunity to help others! The greatest thing I can conceive of at the moment.

Later on in the evening Joan talked to someone who gave us a list of several local people whose cancer had been eliminated by macrobiotics, so the hope starts to build again, slowly, piece by piece. Why do we always seem to require more and more proof instead of just trusting in God's will?

6 July 1990

Not surprisingly I spent quite a restless night bothered not only by a headache but also by facial pain in the area of my cheeks and upper back teeth. Part of the cleansing process? Finally at about 0230 I took a percocet (my first pain medicine in several weeks) and shortly went to sleep and remained so until 0545. When awake, I expanded my visualization to include the little people in white coveralls using high pressure hoses and long handled brooms to scrub any black spots off my bones. Not knowing exactly where problem areas might be found, I had to scrub them all—a big job!

Awoke feeling good and left early for 0900 pulmonary test. Due to bad traffic problems, one hour after leaving the boat we had gone less than 10 to 12 miles. So we turned around and came back. The test was rescheduled for the coming Monday.

Felt good and optimistic during the rest of the day. Morning walk was most pleasant and came back feeling strong and refreshed. Meditated up on deck just before lunch but don't know how deeply I went as I really had no sensations. Stepped up frequency of visualization and now that locations of bone cancer are known, I am able to concentrate special attention by sending scrubbing crews in those locations and also direct additional amount of white cells to help out.

In the afternoon Joan talked to the wife of a man who had been in a NIH program for treatment of brain tumors. Before his treatments were completed, NIH judged the program unsuccessful and just put him out on his own, even though he was suffering from serious side effects. He then turned to macrobiotics and has been on it for almost three years. He has experienced steady improvements and his last brain scan showed him to be completely tumor free. He is still suffering from some of his previous side effects but Michael feels this is from his heavy radiation treatment and should also improve as the body continues to cleanse and repair itself. We plan to get together with them for further talk as this is certainly a case where macrobiotics seemed to step in after the best of medical science had failed and helped snatch a life back from the very edge of death.

I keep having this feeling that God's true purpose in my life has not really been revealed yet, but perhaps it is to show that terminal cancer can be defeated. As yet, this message has not come in any brilliant flash of revelation but seems to be building, small bit by small bit. Perhaps this is just wishful thinking on my part—i.e., "Save me from this, dear God, so that I can help others"—but I really don't think so. Still keep having the feeling that it would be very easy to just accept death but these thoughts are not as frequent or as strong as before.

Chapter Nine

Spiritual Calm and an Emotional Roller Coaster

Mark and I were able to talk about spirituality and what we thought happened after death. We both knew it was not the end. I reminded Mark of a quotation from Teilhard de Chardin that says we are not physical beings having a spiritual experience but spiritual beings having a physical experience.

"I do believe our true essence is spirit and that our souls chose planet earth as a schoolhouse—we can choose to incarnate as often as we need to in order to learn our lessons," I told Mark. "When we graduate, I think we get to go on to explore and learn in other dimensions, even other galaxies."

He wondered, "How do I know when it's time to graduate?" I didn't have an answer.

When we were dating Mark told me he was never going to be old. For some reason that stuck in my long-term memory. Maybe he should have been more specific about what he meant by old. When you are in your twenties, sixty seems very old! Or had he known on a soul level his work would be done by then?

Mark's moods swung like a yo-yo. When he was down, I was affected too, and I tried to come up with something to raise his spirits. His journal reveals this constant struggle.

7 July 1990

One month since surgery! Slept well during the night and each time that I did awake, used it as an opportunity to apply visualization. It is getting easier to do and I really feel a part of it. Several times the question of dying came to mind and I got the strong feeling that this is not the path that I am to take. Wonder what tomorrow will produce along this line?

Spent slow day, cleaned boat, and Bonnie and Rodney came out for the afternoon for a breezy visit. Fireworks display at night was nice. No real deep thoughts during day and visualizations not as clear as before. Meditated up on deck and became very peaceful.

8 July 1990

Spent generally restful night and visualized on those occasions I did awaken. At 0500 awoke and was immediately filled with doubts about the value of the entire undertaking. Once as I was drifting back to sleep, I could see the dark path I started to climb after the car accident (my near death experience?) and could somewhat picture the beautiful, sun drenched meadow at the top. I didn't see myself starting to make the climb. Meaning??

Was quite tired during most of the day and spent a lot of time sleeping and resting. Felt good to do so and on several occasions I could feel my body starting to float. During meditation I saw clearly the face of an unknown woman. Also, for a brief span of time, I saw a bright flash of light each time I inhaled and this light traveled down a cone shaped tunnel as I exhaled and finally disappeared as I finished exhaling.

9 July 1990

Awoke at 0430 and went through a period of doubt about how successful this program is going to be and whether I am just fooling myself with false hope. So far I have not read or heard of one case where renal cancer has been defeated. I know I should not need such reassurance if I really believe that a miracle is going to happen in my case but old patterns die hard. Perhaps I am to be the first but then again perhaps not. Only time will tell.

Underwent pulmonary test in the morning and actually did better on several of them than I had done before my lung surgery. Only the diffusion test came out a bit worse.

During afternoon meditation I had four separate visions—two I couldn't recall after I had them but in the final two the following was seen: 1) I was on a dirt bike and successfully made it climb over the end of a flat bed truck. 2) I was on a screened-in porch with a black family, one of whom was a middle-aged woman dressed in a tan dress with white trim and of a style that Aunt Walborg would have worn. Nothing was said or done, I was just there for a brief moment.

Felt generally tired and down for most of the day. No real urge to do anything, even sleep. Hope this loss of energy was due, as predicted, to the new diet plan and that energy levels will increase soon.

10 July 1990

Awoke again about 0400 feeling very doubtful and listless. Didn't really want to get out of bed and go for my morning meditation session with Jim or Reiki session with Merrill and Jean.

Two-hour session with Jim went well. We discussed a range of subjects relevant to my illness and how to cope with it and life in general. Time went very fast.

Session with the Whitmans was, as usual, very relaxing and I felt great heat being transmitted to my upper chest area by the person who had placed their hands in that location. (Jean, I believe, even though her hands normally are very cool feeling.)

During our post-treatment talks, I started to feel energy starting to return and by the time we were ready to leave, I really wanted to do the driving. This was in complete contrast to the trip in where I didn't feel that I had the energy necessary to get us safely into town and was glad to let Joan drive.

Rest of day went quite well and energy levels seemed to stay up. Meditation session was interrupted by Poozie wanting to play so nothing happened during that session.

Began to realize that before I found out that cancer had entered my bones, I really felt that I was totally clean and that it would be quite a straight forward and relatively easy task to keep it from ever returning. Almost like I felt after my kidney was removed—"Well, that's taken care of and is behind me! On with the next thirty years of life." I know now that up until I found out I wasn't clean, I really thought I had it made, even though I went through bouts of trying to deal with my possible death. I am now starting to realize (and admit honestly) that even under the best circumstances I probably don't have a long period of time left here on earth. I know that if I really expected a healing miracle I could live to be a very old man and should just expect and accept this. However, since old ways die hard, I find I have a tough time accepting this on simple faith when my logical mind tells me that statistically this just isn't going to happen. The odds are totally against it . . . why should it happen to me? Guess it has been said before, "Oh ye of little faith."

11 July 1990

Awoke off and on during the night but every time I would start to get some thoughts strung together, I would fall asleep again. Just before I got up I tried to meditate but about the time I was completely relaxed and ready, my legs shot up by themselves and thus ended that little undertaking.

After getting up I started thinking more and more about yesterday's thoughts about my possible death, the timing thereof and my overall chances for beating an early departure. The more I thought, the more the following seemed to become clearer: Like it or not, admit it or not, at first I must have looked at macrobiotics as being the magic bullet that was going to do in my cancer. After all, hadn't it worked for others in far worse shape than me? This is mainly what we have been given so far—those cases where it has worked.

Now, what about those cases where it didn't work? I really didn't want to think about the latter but I am sure that these cases far outweigh those of success. Easy answer, eat macrobiotic and live to a ripe old age. I am sure that nothing is going to be this simple and am becoming more convinced that I had better stop concentrating on just having more time to live and start concentrating on improving the quality of the time I do have left, be it measured in months or years.

Spent most of the day by myself as Joan went with a friend to help her cope with her having had to put her very ill father in a nursing home. On her big day away she gets to trade one set of problems for another.

Took a long walk in the morning and it felt very good. Decided that I am going to have to stop letting this cancer problem totally consume my thoughts and time. My new approach now is going to be one of doing everything I can to help heal myself and then just let what happens happen.

As a start I drew separate septic plans for each of our twelve Rock Hill lots to submit to the State Health Department for septic permits. Felt good and I really gave very little thought to my health problem. Hope I can keep it up!

12 July 1990

Spent a restful night and visualized on those occasions when I awoke. Good carryover from the previous day!

Left for the healing service in Baltimore feeling very optimistic and fully expecting something wonderful to happen. Just after sitting down in the church I closed my eyes and immediately got the feeling of an unknown presence enveloping me. I could just feel it almost wrapping itself totally around me and the result was one of wonder and awe. Taking this as a great sign, I asked God to give me a vision of my future and immediately an extremely clear and detailed picture of me dressed in a light blue suit and lying in a coffin was received. Shocked at this I said that I won't accept it and blanked it out of my mind. I then asked again for a vision of my future and again the same clear picture of me in my coffin came into view. This time I was tempted to look closely at my face to see how old I appeared to be but I didn't. Again I said that I won't accept this and mentally wiped it from my mind. A third time I asked for a vision and this time a clear picture of Joan in a white wedding dress, running forward and looking up at an angle immediately flashed on my mental screen.

This ended my visionary requests and left me feeling very down. I had come with a very positive feeling that something wonderful was going to happen to me and now this.

Needless to say, the rest of the service was a very emotional experience and by the time the minister laid his hand on me, my insides hurt deeply and I felt as if some foreign object was being driven through them.

The trip home was rather a quiet affair and I was glad for the opportunity to drive and take my mind off of what I had just experienced.

Sometime after arriving home I related my experiences to Joan who, as usual, tried to explain them in the most positive light. Meditations followed and though I went into deep relaxation, nothing of a visionary nature appeared.

I then went for a long walk and at about the halfway point a severe thunder storm started rolling in. It was truly awesome and exciting to watch this powerful force approaching and as I walked and heard the thunder boom and roll, I got very excited and thought that if this is my time to leave this earth I am going to try and come back as a Thunder God. What fun—just me and the old Vikings.

After beating the storm home I found that Joan had made several phone calls regarding my earlier visions and the most informed individual (Rita Dwyer, past president of the Association for the Study of Dreams) said that rarely do such visions or dreams deal with the person's own death but usually have other meanings. After getting all the details she said that she saw this perhaps as being the death of my old self and a time for my new self to come forth. She even saw Joan in a wedding dress as portraying our new life together; a time to go back and renew the joys we experienced when we were first married. Sure sounds better than my first thoughts on the subject.

13 July 1990

Slept well and even though I was awake from 0430 to 0530, this time period was spent in somewhat hazy visualizations. Am going to have to jazz up my approach to breathe some new life into the program.

Afternoon meditation was a bit different in that I had a hard time in blanking out my mind and had a series of very clear visions of scenes from marine boot camp days. Finally got my mind to settle down but achieved only peace and quiet.

In the evening went to a macrobiotics dinner and lecture by Lino Stanchich. Food was quite good and dessert (my first real one) was most delicious. Must have eaten too much as stomach acted up a bit. Probably ate something deadly! Lino's lecture emphasized the importance of chewing so we are now going to chew each mouthful 150 times with our breakfasts as suggested. He also said he is not aware of any of his patients with cancer that has lived while cooking with electricity, a chaotic energy. Will have to check this one out with Michael.

Met and talked to the woman whose husband recovered completely from brain tumors (NIH had given up on him) after going on macrobiotics. Interesting conversation and will try to have them out to the boat soon to continue it. Also met a most gracious and delightful individual, whose oncologist suggested she try macrobiotics after everything else had failed to stop her breast cancer. Will contact her oncologist for an appointment and advice on NIH program.

14 July 1990

Ate first breakfast with 150 chews. Long way to spend a morning but must admit it was restful and quiet, almost like meditating.

Rest of the day just sort of happened. Didn't feel real up or down just rather empty. Am really starting to question the worth of everything I am trying to do as it sometimes seems so puny in relationship to the cancer I am involved with. Perhaps just grasping at straws but I guess that is all that there is. Why can't I just learn to trust in God's will? Could be that I feel that what He wants and what I want are not the same? Keep asking myself why, if God wants me to beat this cancer and live, am I filled with so many doubts?

Received a call from a man from the Full Gospel Business Men's Association, who had been contacted by my sister Dussie. He related his own story of miraculous healing some 27 years ago and then, after having me repeat after him a prepared type of confession, prayed for me to be healed. It still bothers me that people believe that they have to put words in other people's mouths before that individual can talk to God in "the right way." Know I shouldn't think such thoughts, but they are there. Was thankful for his concern and even though he equated my cancer to the work of the Devil, I felt he was very sincere in what he was doing. Was very nice of Dussie to show the depth of her concern and love in this way.

We picked up some videos at the Baltimore healing service. Mark found Bernie Siegel's tape "Fight for Your Life" to be helpful. Siegel points out there is always hope—that hope is hope and there is no such thing as false hope. Mark had not been interested in listening to Siegel a year ago when he spoke at the center I helped create. Now Mark was ready to listen.

15 July 1990

Went to bed at midnight and then didn't sleep very well. Awoke several times and each time tried my visualization but was very difficult to do and I didn't feel that I was doing much, if any, good. From 0430 I laid awake until almost 0600 just feeling very depressed. Nothing I did to try and shake it worked and thankfully I finally went back to sleep. Slept until about 0645 at which time I felt the need to get up and do something, so here I sit writing.

Breakthrough (hopefully)! Watched Bernie Siegel's video "Fight for Your Life," which dealt with cancer survivors. One of the first things I heard was the statement that all cancers have been beaten, and that really got my attention. First I have heard of someone surviving renal cancer. Everything in the film made good sense and I realized that I have to shift emphasis completely away from dying (which is certainly one possibility) to that of living, which is well worth fighting all out for.

Much emphasis was placed on obtaining the best medical help and make certain that they are only one part of a team that is going to help you survive. You, however, are the most important factor in whether you are going to make it, and it will be a long tough fight. The video emphasized the importance of meditation and visualization in this healing process and stressed that you have to take charge of this disease and not let it take charge of you. Keep an absolutely positive attitude that you are going to beat it and don't waste time on negative thoughts as you don't have time for them. Keep believing that if only one person is to survive your type of cancer, you will be that person. Tough to do? Absolutely, but well worth the effort.

Everything just seemed to slip in place, and I really feel that I am on the right track to victory. Even the importance of my changed diet seemed to make absolute sense, for food has always been such an important part of my life that being willing to completely change what and how I eat must, to me, represent my total commitment to winning this battle. Yet I now know that it is but one element and well may not even be one of the most important one (none of the survivors even mentioned diet or changed eating habits) but if I think that it is important then IT IS! Was most interesting to listen to Dr. Bernie Siegel blast the medical profession for their mostly uncaring methods of treating patients, especially their "I'm the doctor. Do what I say," rather than "Let's work together to make you whole again."

16 July 1990

Went in for my EKG stress test at 0900 and found a most delightful group of technicians to work with. End results showed that I might have partial blockage of my main heart arteries though the attending doctor said that based on how well I did on other portions of the test he thought that the machine might be giving a "wrong positive reading." He went on to say that such readings are quite common in my age group and that further testing would be required to see what's what. It is now up to Drs. Monty and Anders to request the test, so I will probably not even hear from the dynamic duo unless I call them.

Contacted a recommended oncologist and will go in to interview her next Tuesday. If I don't like either her or her approach to my problem, I will keep searching.

17 July 1990

Again awoke about 0430 but felt very rested. Dozed and visualized until time to get up. Regarding visualization, I am back to using mainly the little men in white with high pressure hoses and an occasional long handled scrub brush to clean up my affected areas. The old vision of a machine turning out white cells that I directed to different parts of my body just didn't seem to work anymore and this really does. At times I also visualize white cells zapping any black cancer cells they may come across and at times larger killer cells are sent into specific areas just to check them out. Perhaps the above change is based on my body telling me that more white cells are not needed at this time.

Strange things started happening yesterday after my stress test. First of all I started to feel much more optimistic about my chances for success even in the face of what could ultimately be bad news regarding the condition of my heart. This feeling kept growing during the day and by late afternoon I was on a positive high. This feeling continued throughout the night and as I sit here writing this at 0820, I still feel wonderful. I am going to win, no doubt about it!

The second thing that started happening was that my energy level seemed to start increasing and again by late afternoon I felt as full of pep and vigor as I can recall feeling for months. This feeling also remains with me this morning and in general, I just feel great about myself and what I have to do.

Session with Jean and Merrill again was a good experience and the conversation rewarding. Though I can't honestly say that I feel the infusion of any healing power, I always leave their session feeling very relaxed. My super high feeling of the previous afternoon and this morning started to diminish somewhat during the afternoon. I still felt generally optimistic but at a somewhat reduced level.

18 July 1990

Awoke about 0330 and though I only dozed off from that point onward, I did use the time for a series of visualizations. Note: Weighed in at Jean and Merrill's on the 17th and found I had lost another 4 pounds. Now down to 176 and hope I can hold it there.

It seems that the soreness in my right center chest area is getting a bit worse or perhaps not any better. Hope this is just due to the fact that the previous sore spots at the front and back hinge points of the rib cage have gotten much better and this now just seems to be worse by comparison. Hope Dr. Gomes will say that soreness is in the area where the rib spreader was attached and such pain is due to the bruising that occurred. The one thing I don't want to hear is that it is probably due to the bone cancer getting worse.

During one of my awake periods last night I thought about my problem and the enormity of what I am trying to do became very real. I (we) are trying to prove medical science wrong and cure a disease I have been told is basically untreatable. I'm starting to get a better feel of how hard this fight will be and that it will take every resource I can muster plus many more from other sources if I am to succeed. Looking at it in this way can really shake your confidence.

20 July 1990

Slept well until about 0630 but guess that this was due more to having stayed active until after midnight than any other factor. Feel quite refreshed this morning and overall energy levels seem to be staying up. First solo trip to Stafford coming up and I am looking forward to meeting with Showke.

Trip to Stafford went well and had a good meeting with Showke. Told him about my condition and what I am doing about it and he was very supportive. He was specially interested in the macrobiotic diet and said he thought that was the way people were meant to eat. He requested any info I can provide him on it and said they already eat many of the foods I described.

Traffic coming and going was heavy but I didn't let it get to me and I arrived home without my usual headache. Real progress! I have not taken any aspirin in weeks. System must really love this.

After Mark's head injury in the car accident as a child, the doctor told him then he would probably experience headaches for the rest of his life. And, until now, he had.

Meditation period was quite short (about 20 minutes) but very restful. No vision received but even so, I look forward to this period daily—quality time.

Each day I become more thankful for the wonderful and total support I am getting from Joan. Don't know how I could go through what I am going through without her at my side. I can't adequately express how much her total participation means to me but all I know is that I couldn't make it without her!

Energy levels remain good and my positive outlook for total success continues to grow.

21 July 1990

Slept very well and spent very little time awake. Feel very good and ready to meet the day. Believe I am really starting to live much more in the now and the quality of life is definitely improving.

Went to the Machodoc Creek home owners association meeting at Joe and Betty's house and learned that Betty is a cancer survivor. She had breast cancer and after surgery had no further treatments and just made up her mind that she was going to live. She told me that she once saw one of her doctors who was amazed to still see her alive. He told her she should have been dead months ago.

Afternoon meditation again produced nothing but restfulness though the half hour thus spent seemed to go by in just a few minutes. Must have been deeper than I realized. Continued to feel good and optimistic during rest of day and energy level stayed high. Washed entire boat in the heat—three hours—without it really tiring me.

Chapter Ten

New Hopes and Old Fears

24 July 1990

Awoke at 0430 and suddenly the enormity of what I am trying to do really hit me. In the face of all the evidence today I really questioned whether my puny efforts are worth anything and if I am only fooling myself. The thoughts lasted for about an hour despite my best efforts to overcome them.

At 0530 I tried to visualize, something that hadn't been very successful previously during the night, and as soon as I started, I felt as if an electric charge was running through my body. No vision occurred but I could almost feel my good cells being vitalized. A bit later I again tried to visualize and the same thing happened and left me with a very good feeling. Sometime later, I tried it for a third time and though I didn't feel any electric charge, I felt a sort of warm glow spreading over my mid section, which again left me feeling quite optimistic and good.

Had an appointment with Dr. Voith, a new oncologist, in the afternoon. She turned out to be everything the previous two oncologists were not, i.e., warm, understanding and very humanistic. Best news received was that after reviewing my bone and CAT scans, she did not feel that they showed positive proof that cancer had spread to my bones. She ordered new bone X-rays and blood work and hopes to tell more from these. Don't want to get hopes up too high but news sure made me feel good.

25 July 1990

Slept well last night and even when I awoke quite early, felt very relaxed and wonderfully comfortable just lying in bed. Great feeling from yesterday is still with me and only hope and pray that I am not setting myself up for a great letdown.

Went to my first cancer survivors' support group at the Institute for Attitudinal Studies and though it was their last meeting of the summer and thus sort of a wind down session, it was quite interesting. Group has been together for quite a while but I felt very much at ease with them. I was the only male member and feel that I will have to attend a few more fall sessions to see if it is the right group for me. Wednesday morning meeting time could be a bit of a problem in the future.

In the afternoon I received a call from Dr. Voith saying that bone X-rays and two blood tests all support her previous diagnosis that there does not appear to be any clear evidence of bone cancer or other active cancer activity in my body at this time. Third blood test could indicate otherwise but its results are not in yet. She believes shoulder spots are due to arthritis and rib spots due to post operative trauma. What wonderful news. Rest of the day was spent on a tremendous emotional high. Really felt like going out and having a very large pizza!

Joan attended her first macrobiotic cooking class in the evening and came back full of ideas for more delicious food. The day was complete!

26 July 1990

Slept very well last night and even upon awakening at 0430 couldn't finish a visualization session as I kept falling asleep. Just before getting up I started to wonder if this could just be another of cancer's cruel tricks of seeming to go away only to come back at you again more powerful than ever in other places. Have to stop thinking this way and really concentrate on living in the now which, at this exact moment, is very wonderful.

Attended healing services in Baltimore and for a second week in a row, didn't really feel that I got much out of it. We arrived just as the service was starting and so didn't have a chance to get in the proper mood.

Afternoon meditation was again a very peaceful and relaxing period of time. Had a vision of a black man talking but couldn't recall what he said. Though time periods spent seem to be somewhat less, now down to about twenty minutes, I really look forward to them and feel that they have become a real part of my daily routine.

Have noticed over the past two weeks that I have been getting lightheaded whenever I stand up quickly. This has become more frequent and I hope it is due to my weight loss rather than anything to do with cancer.

27 July 1990

Old habits die hard! During my early morning awake time I found my mind going over many old financial and other concerns—what if the boat and building lots don't sell; what if the house in Florida doesn't sell; problems of packing and moving furniture back; what if the boat has further blister problems, etc., etc. Try as I might, I couldn't erase these thoughts and just as soon as I would get rid of one, another would pop into my thoughts. It was aggravating to find that on one of the first mornings that my mind was free of cancer concerns, (relatively), these other negative thought patterns would so easily return. Tried the now approach but somehow even this didn't work. Too bad, for it really ruined what should have been quality time and left me feeling quite depressed.

Funny how it seems almost easier to deal with the realities of cancer than the vagaries of "what ifs" in the future and "should haves" of the past.

Afternoon meditation was very good and had gone very deep when Poozie decided to jump up and join us. Brought me out of it and I was unable to return to the deep level again. Too bad because who knows what I might have been experienced had I remained in that state for a longer time.

Still have the feeling that I am cancer-free as of this time.

28 July 1990

Awoke at 0300 and really beat myself up for the next three hours on the same types of problems and worries confronted yesterday morning. It was a very bad time period and nothing that I tried to break out of it worked. Kept blaming myself for developing the lots and buying the house in Florida and all the other money spent last year with the resultant reduction in our reserves. It made me almost sick. No matter how I tried to put it out of my mind, it kept coming back to be looked at from another angle, then another angle, then another angle, etc., etc. The next projection dealt with the future and the fact that I am now earning nothing, the lots probably won't sell, the boat probably won't sell (realistically) the sale of the house in Florida is questionable and yet our level of expenditures continues to be high.

I tried to shut it off by trying to turn it over to God, but it seemed as if He didn't want any part of it. Even Joan's assurances that "everything will work out just fine," seemed to be very naive and not really facing up to or realizing the severity of the situation. Even saying "Stop it, you're helping to kill yourself" didn't work. My mind seemed to have taken complete control of the situation. Nothing that I could do would bring it back under my control. This then brought on another round of "Perhaps you really want to die as a way to solve your problems" thoughts, to which I could truly answer (at times shout) no, no, no!

All in all, it was a most unpleasant time, yet almost as if by magic, at around 0600 all the above left me and I felt somehow very optimistic and good. Can't explain why but just did. Hope the above won't repeat itself again. Still feel as if I am cancer-free but wonder how long this will continue if I have many more bad night sessions. Hopefully all this is due to my diet change and not to the fact that I really haven't learned anything from what I have been through or am not really a changed person at all.

Rest of the day went well and good feeling remained. Had nice half hour meditation and had a vision of people talking early on but couldn't recall any details when meditation ended. Reading and nice walk ended the day's activities.

I had decided the quality time Mark and I could spend together was much more important than money. I knew he was concerned we were living off our savings. But I felt our full-time job was healing. We had to give it our best shot. If he was not to be cured of cancer, he wouldn't even have a retirement. It was better we use those funds to live now. He, of course, wanted me to be well provided for, and I tried to reassure him I could always go back to work full-time. Working full-time now, commuting and trying to continue our healing program in an attitude of peace and calm, would be very stressful. Living with less money was my choice. Mark didn't like to hear platitudes like "the universe will provide," but I've always trusted that it will.

29 July 1990

Slept very well during the night and even though I did wake up at 0300, no negative thought patterns occurred and I went back to sleep. Had good visualization session just before getting up. Since I feel I am cancer-free at this time, I have had to change my visualizations and instead of the good white cells absorbing black cancer cells, they now occasionally come across a questionable gray cell and do away with it. Hose and brush crews are busy keeping me clean and well scrubbed internally. I travel throughout my entire system in a white cell vehicle that has a viewing dome on top. Several times a day I run my white cells through a revitalization machine and sent them back to do their jobs. Must admit that since I feel I am cancer-free, I want to get lazy and slack off on visualizations but realize I must keep them going.

Spent a lazy Sunday and went to dinner at Patty and Gastons. Had a good time and Patty cooked special food separately for us—plain lobster, brown rice, and steamed vegetables without salt. Very dear of her to do so.

Mark continued to work on his visualizations, but often he hit a slump. It bothered him when the imagery was not as clear as it had been previously. We continued with Reiki, which he said was ". . . very relaxing and peaceful—I wish it could last longer." Mark agreed to oversee a construction project in Stafford, Virginia, so he started a long commute every day. Even so, he always took time to meditate daily. He was amazed he could remain calm in heavy traffic, and he even found the drive very relaxing, saying, "That is one thing I have learned how to do from all of this."

His only major area of frustration had to do with his not receiving any clear guidance regarding his future direction of activity or work, which he felt should be something more meaningful than what he was doing. When we lived in a house, Mark had always kept busy with projects: building furniture, a new deck, a gazebo. When he ran out of projects, we'd sell the house and buy or build a new one. We had moved fifteen times. Now, without any "hands-on" projects, he had time to think and reflect on what was really important, to discover his mission. In his journal he stated, "I feel that I am now totally open to whatever purpose

God may intend for my remaining years. Lacking firm direction, I just seem to be marking time. I feel the need to really get involved in something but that 'something' totally eludes me and this is really starting to bother me."

7 August 1990

Slept quite well and had a wonderful dream where I was hang gliding for what seemed like hours. Had a marvelous time of it as I soared through the trees and over the rivers and hills. Landed safely after flying through a storm and wished it could have continued. Awoke at 0400 and really worked on my visualizations. Not too successful but was able to see work being done on my right shoulder and right rib area plus general patrol and maintenance on the rest of my body.

Had an appointment with Dr. Voith and found out that all my blood work indicated no active cancer at this time. She was, however, very suspicious of a spot on my right lung which could either be post operative trauma or some evidence of new cancer activity. She did say that active cancer is something I will have to face at some time in the future but for now I appear to be fine. She has scheduled me for monthly blood work and chest X-rays plus a CAT scan every three months.

Meditation period was not as restful as most but did last almost thirty minutes. Visualizations still lack clarity and are very hard to concentrate on even though I now know that I must focus on my right lung. All in all, a very nice day. Contacted American Cancer Society about becoming a volunteer.

We sold a building lot and I hoped that would lessen Mark's concern about finances. When he awoke during the night, he concentrated on his visualizations and finally achieved better results when: "I envisioned my right lung spot as being a light gray spongy material which I scooped out by hand and fed to my hungry white cells who loved it."

10 August 1990

Slept well and felt very rested even though I woke up a number of times during the night. Used the 0300 wake up for deep breathing and visualization. Also visualized briefly during other such periods as well. At about 0430 I felt so good and optimistic that I felt like I should get up and do something. Fortunately the feeling passed!

Afternoon meditation was interrupted after eighteen minutes by a phone call from the doctor with the results of my last stress test which showed that I have had a heart attack at some point in time. He said it could have occurred during surgery or could have been a "silent attack" but as a result, I do not qualify for the NIH program. At least this eliminates having to make that decision. Wonder if it could have happened that one night in the hospital when I got up in the middle of the night and went for a walk during which my heart really started to race and pound. I had the nurse check it, but she didn't think the elevated pulse rate was significant enough to get the duty intern. Guess I will never know for sure.

Remainder of day was sort of so-so; I didn't feel either real up or down. Made me realize, however, that it now appears to be totally up to me/us to lick this thing as we don't seem to be able to look to medical science for much (if any) help. Visualization up to the phone call were very clear and strong but diminished in both after getting the news.

12 August 1990

Went to bed very late and awoke early. Felt rested, however. Perhaps we need less sleep on this diet. Visualized several times during the night and though I could develop the desired pictures, they were not very strong or convincing.

Spent another lazy Sunday morning reading and then took Teresa and Kris to an early movie to celebrate Teresa's 27th birthday. Doesn't seem possible she can be that old. Wonderful to have both girls so close and enjoy their company greatly.

Spent entire afternoon with girls and got home just in time for a late meal and a walk. Didn't meditate or work out and may use Sundays as my whole day off from regular routines. Felt good all day and spirit was high. Talked to Seattle bunch and again was touched by their expressions of concern and love.

Chapter Eleven

Macro-Mellow Mark

Mark's journal entries became shorter and more standardized as he seemed to get back on a routine with fewer peaks and valleys. In the fall of 1990, he stopped writing in a journal altogether.

More and more of Mark's days were upbeat without worries or concerns. He was proud of his progress on handling stress and almost totally overcoming negative thoughts. He continued to drive the long distance to his job site without the traffic getting him angry or upset. And no headaches! We laughed about how he was becoming "macro-mellow." The shift was amazing.

After reading *Healing Visualizations* by Gerald Epstein, M.D., Mark modified his visualization techniques. Epstein says that the amount of time you spend on each session is not as important as the intensity of what you see and feel. Less can be more, so short three- to five-minute sessions many times a day could work as well as one long session. When Mark started to do this, his visualizations were, as he said, "clear and very spirited." One session was extremely vivid and powerful, and his whole body seemed to tingle and his pulse rate increased as he envisioned the healthy white cells racing through his system doing their clean up work.

I continued to do Reiki energy work on him every day, usually for forty-five minutes to an hour. It was a very peaceful time and our souls seemed to merge on a deep level; we really felt united as one during these sessions.

We continued our Monday Reiki sessions with Jean and Merrill as well, and Mark always felt better afterwards. Sometimes he would feel extreme heat being generated, as though there were hot spots in one of our palms, which passed heat directly to him. Sometimes one of us would receive a vision during the session and afterwards we'd talk about what it might mean. Once Jean said she saw a beam of light flowing from her down the length of her body. Another time she saw Mark standing before her as a powerful Native American warrior. Merrill often saw and felt others he assumed were spirit guides.

Mostly Mark felt very relaxed after the sessions. I've often thought that if nothing else, the person on the table receives an hour of being the recipient of unconditional love from people who truly care and want to help. Humans crave touch of this caliber.

We had our annual Odd Couples Party on our boat and took fourteen couples for a cruise and dinner on the bay. This tradition started a few years earlier when we were musing with friends and neighbors how unique it was that so many of us had been married to the same partner for twenty-five years or more. In this day and age, it seems odd. "Membership" in this "club" required a quarter-century marriage. We even elected officers. I was always re-elected social secretary to ensure the ritual of the annual cruise. No one seemed to mind the food was all macrobiotic this year. Margaret and Roy, our friends who were married the longest, were co-presidents. We all wondered if Margaret would be alive next year. Her head was bald from chemotherapy and she was careful to sit in the shade. As the crowd celebrated our many years of friendship, I wondered how many thought that Mark, too, might soon leave the group.

But mostly we savored each day as it came and went, enjoying gorgeous late summer weather on the bay, sailing and fishing with friends. People raved about how good our macrobiotic food tasted. Mark felt good about that as he didn't want people feeling sorry for him having a restricted diet. I'm not sure he ever completely got over the feeling that it was a diet of deprivation. He would joke, "If I loved it before, I can't have it now!"

At times Mark noticed before getting up in the morning, he'd feel a very strong almost electric current flowing through his body. Or he would feel a warm glow of energy spread throughout his entire chest area. It was so completely filled with warm energy, he said, "It felt as though my chest was no longer a part of my body but a separate entity unto itself." This feeling seemed to last for quite awhile and then was suddenly gone. He had no idea what all that meant but the experience was very real to him. I hoped it meant healing was taking place. Was it spiritual healing or physical healing—or both?

Three months had passed since Mark had undergone lung surgery, and he was clearly living more fully in the present than ever before. Once, after a three-mile walk, he told me, "Joan, it feels so good to be doing just what we're doing, not thinking either about the future or the past." This realization seemed to be at a new and different level. "It's strange," he said, "the areas in which I walked today were very familiar, but it was almost as if I were really seeing its true beauty and wonder for the first time."

In September 1990, Mark wanted to revisit his childhood home in northern Minnesota and attend his fortieth high school reunion in St. Paul. We planned to have a big reunion with my family as well.

To maintain a strict macrobiotic diet, we had to establish a new travel routine of cooking along the way. Our car was entirely filled up with our food and cooking gear. We carried our camp stove, spring water, pots and pans, and food into the motels where I cooked our meals. This worked out well, although I learned the hard way not to cook right under the smoke detector. During the day, we stopped at rest stops to cook lunch and found the whole affair took about an hour, not much longer than a normal lunch stop at a greasy fast food place. These picnics reminded us of our early camping days.

We drove to Thief River Falls where Mark's father had been a pastor. The old parsonage had been torn down and a new house built on the lot, but the school next door and many of the stores downtown were more or less the same. The day was drizzly and cold as we cooked lunch on the camp stove by the river. The mood was poignantly nostalgic and bittersweet as Mark shared memories of his childhood.

At Mark's fortieth high school reunion in St. Paul, he immediately recognized old friends, many of whom attended school together since the fifth grade. I sensed Mark was proud to introduce me to his old buddies. They reveled in their exploits, and I heard many new stories. For example, Mark and two of his friends would have dinner at each other's house (different times on the same night) and then tell each set of parents that they were staying over at the other friend's house. The parents never suspected that after three dinners, the boys played at Como Park Zoo, climbing into the pens with the buffalo and teasing them until the buffalo charged while the boys nimbly climbed to safety. Finally exhausted, the boys would fall sleep on the park benches.

One of the organizers of the reunion said she thought they should have a reunion every five years. "As we all get older, you never know who will not be alive for the next one." I wondered if they knew Mark had cancer. Would Mark be alive five years from now? Or was this the last time he would be laughing and chatting with his childhood friends?

The rest of the year following Mark's lung surgery was busy and fairly normal. Mark was the general contractor on two office buildings for a friend in Stafford and for the road construction on property owned by another friend. We spent the winter in our home in Florida on the canal where Mark had fun designing and drawing plans for the house we planned to build by a river in the northern neck of Virginia, a lovely area with lots of deer and wild turkey.

Mark and I discovered a spiritualist church where the minister gave everyone a message from Spirit at the close of her sermon. I was happy the very first Sunday Mark and I attended when she said she saw lots of green healing energy flowing from me to Mark. Each service ended with a healing session; Mark always went forward.

Mark was not taking any treatments except to have blood tests every month—all normal—and CAT scans every few months. The latest CAT and bone scans showed the spot on his liver gone, shadow on bone decreased and spot on lung unchanged. We were encouraged. Mark's energy level was good and he rode his bike at least fifteen miles a day; I rode seven. We also spent lazy time on the beach.

While we were in Florida, Mark had a very strange dream. "Last night I had a grand reunion with all the dogs I had as a child. Poozie was whining and barking, wanting to come join us." Mark said he felt bad Poozie couldn't be with him but, he said, "The only way I could figure out how to get her over there was to kill her." Not an option, we agreed.

Chapter Twelve

Bittersweet Days and Dreams

Summer of 1991. We were back in Virginia, staking out our new home site, trying not to take down more trees than necessary. Mark smiled as I asked permission of the trees, apologizing to those that would have to come down and promising them our house would be a place of peace and love.

From the time we bought these 66 riverside acres with a partner in 1972, our family had camped here. Gradually we sold off the lots, never planning to live here ourselves. One lot didn't sell, however, so when we needed it, it was waiting for us.

To be near the construction site, we moved our boat from the Chesapeake Bay to a local marina. One evening at sunset after the workers had left, we sat in the half-constructed house and Mark mused that it was going to be a nice house. "I hope I get to live in it for a few years."

Tiny new spots had been discovered on Mark's right lung. We settled into a routine of going every month to his new oncologist, Dr. Martin, another very caring, competent doctor. While we were in Florida, Dr. Voith had written us with the news she had leukemia and was going into Johns

Hopkins for a bone marrow operation. I'd read where, of physicians, oncologists have the highest rate of cancer and I couldn't help but wonder why. Could it be because oncologists focus on cancer for large portions of their day? Do we get what we focus on? Or is there possibly some sort of "cancer virus" they catch after years of working with cancer patients? Do they have unresolved issues concerning cancer? Or, perhaps, is it because it must be so frustrating and emotionally draining to lose so many of their patients?

After each visit to Dr. Martin and receiving the news that the tumors were slowly growing, we'd drive further on to an appointment with Michael Rossoff, our macrobiotic counselor. He would exam Mark's hands and eyes and take the pulses of the different organs. He'd adjust our diet and tell us things to be encouraged about. We always left feeling optimistic. A little see-saw scenario between Western and Eastern medicine played out each month. Even if macrobiotics was nothing more than a placebo, it was worth the bump up we received after the bad news, leaving us higher than we would have been otherwise.

We were never without hope. There is no order of difficulties in miracles, and we expected a miracle. Even Dr. Martin was impressed at how the tumors seemed to be kept in check, growing so slowly and on some visits showing no growth at all. We explained a little about our macrobiotic diet and the other things we were doing, and Dr. Martin told Mark, "Whatever you are doing, keep on doing it." She even said, "If we had you on an experimental protocol, we'd say it's working."

We listened to Marlo Morgan's tape on her walkabout with aborigines in Australia. They never take nature for granted and each morning have a ceremony to greet the sun. Inspired by the idea, we began a ceremony of greeting the sun with our arms upraised, expressing gratitude for each day before taking our morning walk.

The aborigines also taught Morgan about immortality and the continuity of life after death because they travel between these dimensions at will. They would ask her, "Do you understand forever? It is a *verrrry* long time." We started a new ritual. I'd tell Mark, "I love you forever." Then we'd both nod, smile at one another and say in unison, "Forever is a *verrrry* long time!"

Friends told us about Father Lubey, a retired Catholic priest who held healing services at a church in Oakton. There were accounts of many who had been miraculously healed after his touch. We decided to attend with some of our friends. The church was packed, and we listened to lovely music as even more people squeezed in. Father Lubey spoke about love and we were all moved. One friend, an ex-Catholic (or as she puts it, a "recovering Catholic"), said she had never heard such a message of unconditional love from the pulpit before. There was no mention of the usual sin and guilt. As Father Lubey began the healing service, a row of "catchers" formed behind the people lined up at the altar to receive healing. Apparently, approximately every other person fell backwards after receiving Father Lubey's touch. The fall was called "resting in the spirit." I wondered if Mark would fall back when it was his turn. I figured he would probably resist falling, a macho thing to do. The service continued with more lovely music as Father Lubey shuffled back and forth at the altar, pausing for about thirty seconds with his fingers on the forehead of each person. Many fell backwards. They were allowed to stay down as long as they wanted, and other people just walked around them to take their place at the altar. When it was our turn, Father Lubey stayed almost a minute longer with Mark. Even then, Mark didn't fall. I was next in line and felt myself float backwards, knowing then why they called it "resting with spirit." My catcher gently lowered me to the floor. I felt incredibly peaceful and falling felt just like the natural thing to do.

That night I dreamed Mark was driving a big truck and I was outside standing in front of his cab using hand motions to guide him through a sharp turn in a tight intersection. He made the turn safely and I awoke with the thought, "He's turned the corner!"

Mark also had a dream. At a big reunion of both of our families, he was swimming with a little submarine under water. Then we were in a big A-frame house and someone asked if he wanted to take communion. He said, "Yes." They said, "We'll go get the snakes." They returned with two big black snakes and held them under their feet. They gave Mark and me two pieces of cheese to feed the snakes. They asked Mark, "Do you want to embrace the serpent?" Mark said, "I don't think so." Then one snake reared back and smiled, stretched forward and kissed Mark on the mouth. After that Mark discovered he could fly! Some of the rest of us could too, but Mark could fly the best. He swooped freely turning somersaults. Then he flew higher and higher. We called for him to come back but he kept on flying upwards and away.

I was excited with my dream, thinking there might have been a physical healing. When Mark told me his dream, I wondered if perhaps the healing was spiritual rather than physical.

A couple of days later a letter arrived from my sister Marian who said she'd had a very real dream where Mark was sailing and just continued to sail out of sight even though we were all calling to him to come back. She said she called so loudly to him she woke herself up. She cautioned, "I hope he isn't going out sailing anytime soon," giving a literal interpretation to her dream. I began to wonder if Mark was busy on the astral level at night letting family members know he was getting ready to make his transition.

On Halloween day 1991, we moved from our boat into our new house. We were able to bring all our belongings out of storage where some of them had been for several years. We had fun placing the pictures and art objects around the house, each reminding us of our travels around the world. But they were just things; and after looking at them,

I could just as easily have stored them away again. The simplicity of our lives on the boat had been a cleansing experience. Cancer had reaffirmed to us that material objects are not what is important in life.

Life continued a fairly normal course. Poozie seemed happy to be in a home that didn't move. She curled up on Mark's lap every time he sat down. And once again we had a new community to explore. Mark heard about a poor local family whose home had burned down, so he and some men from church got together and built them a new house. One of the men commented to me, "Your husband can outwork all of us." They didn't even realize that Mark had cancer.

Although I am interested in reincarnation, I'd never been particularly interested in discovering anything about my own past lives. I surprised myself when I signed up for a past life regression with Coletta Long, a highly qualified psychologist who presented a Spiritual Frontiers Fellowship program on reincarnation. When I told Mark, he volunteered, "Maybe the session was meant for me?" I thought, "Of course!" At the same time, I was surprised Mark was interested.

He went to two sessions. There seemed to be no major breakthrough of past life experiences that would explain his cancer, but the regressions did help us understand a couple of important things. During one regression, he was asked to tell where he saw the cancer and when it first started. He saw the cancer starting to form as a dark mass in his kidney at the time when his boss died. He also saw it during a period when he was under a lot of job-related stress.

Although he recalled two past lives, there was no significant revelation. Instead he went back to life between lives, the lovely meadow of his childhood near-death experience. He seemed to prefer to re-experience that state of being rather than a past life.

My niece, a co-chair of the Midwest Spiritual Frontiers Fellowship Retreat, invited me to be a presenter in July and invited Mark to lead an evening rap session on living with cancer. We accepted.

Before we left on this trip to Minnesota, Mark had a long, serious talk with Poozie. She stood in his lap with her paws on his chest as he rubbed her behind her ears. They looked deep into each other's eyes, but I couldn't hear what Mark was saying to her. After we dropped her off at the neighbors who were going to take care of her while we were gone, Mark asked suddenly, "I wonder which of us will die first, Poozie or me?"

I marveled at how Mark's views had changed about these retreats. He was eager to share his experiences if he could help someone else living with cancer. He even attended sessions on UFOs and didn't judge the presenter or the participants. My sister, Mayva, attended the retreat, too, so it was a good time to be with family.

After the retreat, as we were sitting around the kitchen table at Mayva's, someone commented, "You are never free until your kids are out of college and your dog dies." At that moment the phone rang. It was our neighbor. Poozie had just died of a heart attack. I was shocked, but Mark said, "I've been expecting it." When we returned to Virginia, Mark buried her under a large oak tree. Mark, who had always preferred big dogs, once scoffed, "That is not a dog" when he saw the tiny puppy Kristen and I brought home. Now he tenderly made her a headstone that read:

Poozie
1992
Total Love

After our Minnesota trip, we had an appointment with Mark's oncologist. Dr. Martin suggested we see Dr. Hawkins who had spent several years at NIH, participated in the most recent renal cancer research, and was familiar with the newest treatments. We both liked Dr. Hawkins immediately, a big, friendly man with red hair, great warmth, compassion, and sense of humor. He and Mark were soon bantering back and forth easily. He gave us three options: First, we could do nothing. Or we could take the stress tests again to see if Mark's heart could stand the very strenuous experimental treatment of interleukin-2, which required a week in intensive care, a week off, then another week in intensive care. The ICU monitoring was necessary because very high doses of interleukin-2 affect blood pressure, causing fluids to leak into tissue as well as other side effects. Patients who are strong enough might get three rounds of this treatment. Statistically, of those who had taken this treatment, five percent showed a complete regression of all cancer and ten percent showed a partial shrinkage of tumors. There was also a two percent mortality rate, usually from infections. Our third option was for Mark to get a lower dose of interleukin-2 with alfa interferon, injected under the skin as an outpatient. We were told these drugs are supposed to stimulate the immune system.

Dr. Hawkins explained carefully that "about fifty percent of our patients choose the massive dose in the intensive care unit, although other doctors believe the lower dose works just as well and certainly it is not as hard on the body."

"What would you do if you were the one with cancer?" asked Mark. Dr. Hawkins looked thoughtful, "I'd go for it with the intensive care." He never urged Mark to choose any one of the options, but gave him all the information needed to support him in deciding for himself.

"How much time do I have left?" Mark wondered.

Dr. Hawkins looked at us compassionately. "Even if you put a gun to my head, I couldn't tell you. I'm not God."

We decided to delay the decision but to complete the CAT scan and heart stress tests so we'd know if Mark's heart could withstand the extreme treatment.

And we decided to travel. First we visited Mark's two sisters and their families in Seattle for a couple of weeks. I took a suitcase loaded with foods—miso, nori, and sea vegetables—only to discover there was a fine health food store a few blocks away from where we were staying. I cooked for everyone and replenished our supplies for our trip to visit my college roommate Leslie and her husband Harry in Hawaii.

While in Oahu, Leslie knocked on our bedroom door one morning at five-thirty to tell us that a hurricane was headed toward us. Mark and Harry hurried to the store to buy bottled gas, candles, and batteries while Leslie and I monitored news bulletins. The men returned empty-handed after two hours; others had swooped up the commodities. They chuckled over what they saw in carts in the long checkout lines: some carts were full of beer and one woman bought a large bag of briquettes even though she didn't have a barbecue. Leslie laughed. "Thank goodness Harry didn't forget my chocolate candy bars!"

We started securing the house by taping windows. I cooked a huge pot of brown rice in anticipation of the electricity going out. Leslie filled bathtubs and every other large container, including garbage cans, with water. Finally, with the hurricane an hour away, we could only wait. Leslie and I tried to decide whether we should hole up in the windowless laundry room or in the bathroom under a mattress.

Harry and Mark responded differently. Mark shaved and then sat down to read a book; Harry decided it was a good time to organize all of his *Course in Miracles* tapes. Leslie and I discovered the windows in the bedroom were not taped and set to that task. We got silly, laughing at how we all reacted differently to the crisis.

Shortly after the mayor announced the evacuation of the island and while we wondered how that could be accomplished, the hurricane veered off and struck Kauai instead.

A few days later back in Seattle, we explored a park with virgin timber, taking a back road up a mountain. As we came around a curve we suddenly saw Mount Rainier— a snow-capped sacred mountain against a sparkling cloudless blue sky. We stopped to take pictures. Just as I finished our last roll of film, I turned and saw two clouds off to the side we hadn't noticed before. They were saucer shaped like two space ships, one sitting on top of the other. As we looked closer we could see dark shadows, regularly spaced—like windows around the "ships"—showing through the clouds. Two months earlier at the Spiritual Frontiers Fellowship Retreat, we had heard Rauni Luukanen-Kilde, a chief medical officer from Finland, speak about her encounters with UFOs. She showed slides to demonstrate how they often seemed to camouflage the ship in clouds. We sat and watched the clouds _not_ move in the sky for over an hour. But we had no film in the camera!

Chapter Thirteen

Another Kind of Cancer Treatment Begins

27 October 1992—Joan's journal

Scans showed a big change from four and a half to five and a half centimeters on the big tumor and growth on all the others. Previously the growth was gradual and never more than a half centimeter. Now one centimeter growth! Somehow I felt calm with the news and it made it easier to decide on treatment. Then when Michael Rossoff agreed that it was time to go ahead with Western treatment, it was almost with relief. Now I feel that Mark has a good chance of being in the five percent who get a remission. It wasn't until we got home that I could let down and cry—just to release pent up emotions. Mark hugged me and cracked some jokes—saying that the bad news gets easier to accept as time goes on.

Michael Rossoff had told us flying could be very hard on the organs. Since we'd decided to fly on our trip anyway because we felt the psychological boost would be best for us, he'd told us to urinate as soon as we landed "to relieve the kidneys" and to walk barefoot on the soil as soon as we could to ground ourselves and help counter any negative effects. We did these things, but now, the new test results made us wonder if he had been right. Had the unusually rapid tumor growth been activated by the flying?

Mark chose treatment with the lower dose of interleukin-2 and alfa interferon. He was placed in the hospital overnight for observation to see how he handled the first three injections, which were eight hours apart. Mark was not at all hesitant about giving himself shots, and the nurse gave him high marks on his first try.

As a "customer" of the healthcare service, Mark did not give up his rights. When an intern came to take him for a bone scan, Mark sent him away as none had been discussed with Dr. Hawkins. "What difference will it make to know anyway?" asked Mark. "Why put the body through more trauma, especially now when it has trauma enough?" Why indeed? There was a scurry of people in and out to discuss why he should have it and why it had been ordered but Mark was firm and just said, "No." Finally they left us in peace, both of us lying in the hospital bed together. Later, in reaction to the injections, he had severe fever and chills.

Once home, Mark began his new routine—one day, an injection of interleukin-2, the next day, injections of both interleukin-2 and alfa interferon. I constantly assured him I'd be with him every step of the way and he'd say, "We can get through anything because we'll do it together." But when I sat beside him as he gave himself the injections it was difficult for me to watch. He laughed and assured me he could "shoot up" alone. The areas where he injected in his legs and stomach became angry red and so swollen that it became increasingly difficult to find places to inject. But Mark never complained and was even quite analytical about the process. In his precise printing he made a chart of the dates and times for each drug and his reactions, rating the severity of his chills and his temperature. There was also a column for comments, most of which were on his night sweats and when his fevers broke. He hated to wake up clammy and cold and have to change out of a drenched T-shirt. He began to evaluate his nights as to whether they were "two or three T-shirt nights."

During this time Teresa sent Mark a letter.

November 15, 1992

Dear Dad,

I remember when you dropped me off for freshman year at West Virginia University. I was so scared and unsure of myself. I sat in my new surroundings and read the wonderful letter you had written me. As I read about your pride and confidence in me, my fears diminished. How could I be frightened with so much support!

You have always been behind me, and I don't know if you recognize how truly blessed that has made me feel. To know that I could make my own choices in life (including stupid ones) and be secure in the knowledge that my family was behind me.

You have given me so much in my 29 years. From the precious gift of life to advice on which car to buy. What has always impressed me the most is how much you have given of your time and yourself, and the sacrifices you have made for us.

I love and respect you not only as my father, but as a truly admirable person. I hope and pray that we all have lots of years left to spend together. But if that is not the plan, then I will still count myself as one of the lucky ones. For I have known an incredible abundance of love and support— more than most people get in a whole lifetime.

Thank you for my life and for everything you have done for me since August 12, 1963. Whatever happens in the future, I will carry your love with me and will be forever proud and honored to call you my father.

Love always,
Teresa

At the end of five weeks, Mark was exhausted. The mere exertion of taking a shower often put him back to bed for the rest of the morning. He had mouth sores and his tongue was swollen. Nothing tasted good. I'd wait and plan each meal with him to see if I could get some clues about what might be appealing. Then I'd drive to the store to get it. I drove to the store at least twice a day to get such things as tomato soup or chipped beef for creamed beef on toast. None of these were macrobiotic, but "comfort foods" were what tasted good to him now—white crackers, mashed potatoes, and beef gravy. We really went off the diet; we even had ice cream, though I made it with a tofu ice cream mix. As much as possible, I still tried to slip in macro foods.

On the morning of December 18, while I presented a workshop in Fredericksburg, Kristen took Mark for X-rays to find out if the injections had reduced the tumors. They ate dinner with Teresa and then both girls brought him back home. I was reading in the great room and didn't hear them until Mark walked in and stood in front of me with a mock serious expression on his face and said, "Well, the best they could do was almost a fifty percent reduction."

I jumped up and hugged him, tears flowing freely. Through my tears I caught Kristen's happy expression as she came into the room. After five weeks of injections, the X-rays showed a tumor shrinkage from over seven centimeters to just a little over four centimeters. What a Christmas present! And now, the doctor said Mark could have Christmas week off from shots, too. It was our best Christmas ever. Teresa gave us a camcorder; I knew it was because the girls wanted to record their dad on video.

After Christmas, Dr. Hawkins limited the injections to only interleukin-2. After three weeks the X-ray showed only a two-millimeter reduction. Apparently interleukin is more effective when used with alfa interferon. This was disappointing. Dr. Hawkins stopped therapy for two weeks so Mark could gain weight and strength; he would begin with drugs again in February.

During the two-week reprieve, we flew to Arizona for a reunion with Mark's sisters and their families. "The best vacation I've ever had," Mark told his sisters and brother-in-law. They were deeply moved to hear him say this. We also visited several members of my family, and we hiked and played golf. I was amazed at Mark's endurance hiking up Superstition Mountain; I happily carried his clubs for nine holes of golf. The trip provided a much-needed break for both of us. But when we returned, a new set of X-rays showed the tumors had taken another spurt in growth. Once again, I wondered if flying contributed to this.

Chapter Fourteen

Stressed Out and Angry

The stress of cancer brought Mark and me closer together in so many ways. For the two years after the kidney operation, we had avoided thinking about cancer and just had fun together. Cancer returning was an unspoken fear, but we didn't give energy to that thought form.

Two years later, the lung operation sounded a clear wake-up call. It was time to take charge. We threw ourselves into researching alternatives, practicing macrobiotics, meditation, Reiki healing, spiritual healing, and visualization. I put Mark on every prayer list I knew about. I prayed for his highest good, whatever that might be, hoping that it included physical healing. During this time of practicing alternative healing methods Mark felt physically better than he had for many years. We saw, that in some strange way, cancer really was a gift that had strengthened our love and helped teach us to live each moment fully.

Mark and I did everything together. We discussed spiritual issues in depth, including many of the issues I had explored without him since my thirties. He had become open and exploring. We delighted in watching our daughters mature and blossom into fine young women discovering their own walks in life. Whenever Mark wondered if he had accomplished what he was here on planet earth to do, I said, "Just look at Teresa and Kristen. You know you've been a success. Besides how do we ever know if we have finished our mission?"

In November 1992, after four and a half years of cancer, Mark started Western medical treatment. By February 1993, his sense of well-being went rapidly downhill. Now the stress of drug treatment began to drive us apart. Mark no longer felt "macro-mellow;" he felt just plain sick and tired. Little things I did irritated him. He was sarcastic, which irritated me, and I'd feel hurt and angry.

We had tried so hard and had been so hopeful that all the alternatives would heal him. In a voice thick with disappointment, he said, "I guess I was just looking for the silver-bullet approach."

During the first four and a half years of living with cancer, Mark had actively participated in his own healing process, but now it seemed he turned himself over to the doctors to "do it for him." This upset me. I wanted him to try the things Michael Rossoff said could reduce the nausea, such as pressing on acupressure points or drinking ume plum tonic. But I guess when you think you are going to throw up, ume tonic doesn't sound so great. Macrobiotics helped Mark in so many ways: he had no headaches, no gas pains, no hiatal hernia, no irritable bowel syndrome—all the things he'd suffered from before. I felt better on the diet too. Because I still believed it could lessen the drug's side effects, I hated to give it up. Maybe, too, I felt cooking was a tangible way to help and now I felt helpless.

I tried not to be judgmental, not to feel I knew the right answer for Mark. Previously, we meditated together, and during that time I always felt particularly close to him. Now we no longer did this either, and I felt frustrated. It seemed so clear to me all the things we had done helped him feel good during the years of our experiments in healing.

But he gave up all of our alternative healing practices for Western medicine. I wanted him to do both. But the drug treatments were making him sicker, weakening any resolve he had to continue any of it. All he said was, "I've tried all the alternatives, but they don't really seem to be me."

Why is it that someone can do everything and still not be physically healed? Also, aren't there many ways to heal? Mentally, emotionally, and spiritually, as well as physically? I was left with many "don't knows." I had to trust Spirit and be okay with the "don't knows." And, I respected Mark's honesty in doing what felt right for him.

But still, tension built for both of us. Shortly after we returned from Arizona and he resumed interleukin and alfa interferon shots, we fussed at one another over something trivial. Mark said, "Isn't it strange that in Arizona we had such a good time together, but now that we are home we can't stand each other?" It hurt me to hear such a statement from someone I loved so much.

But maybe, too, after all this time we were back at the second stage of death and dying which, according to Elisabeth Kübler-Ross, is anger. The stages don't have to be linear; I think you can bounce back and forth. We were both angry, often at each other. The treatment wiped out Mark's sex drive and that bothered him, too, even though I heard him crack a weak joke to a friend, "There are three things I love in life, good food, a good book, and good sex." Then, he said, "Oh well, one out of three isn't bad—except I don't feel much like reading, either."

I had to back off from trying to keep him trying. I realized I couldn't do it for him and had no right to impose my will. But how I hated to see him suffer so, especially when I still felt strongly our alternative practices could help. I stopped doing Reiki on him except at night in bed when

I'd go to sleep with my hands on his back at the lung energy point. If he didn't feel these things helped, then why should I push him?

So Mark returned to his old world view. I had to make peace with the deeper truth that each of us has to find our own way and that ultimately we learn, through the decisions we make, whatever it is we need to learn. Mark's decision did not make him a failure; he was just very honest in doing what he felt was right for him.

I'd go for walks out into the woods a lot and walk down to the dock to cry. When he lashed out at me, I wanted to shout back, even though we had never before shouted at one another in our marriage. We generally dealt with being upset by withdrawing from one another, for a few hours or even a day, until we regained perspective and could talk or until it no longer seemed important. Now I wanted to shout back at him. When I felt that way, I felt guilty. Mark, after all, was sick; he had every right to be angry. Of course, we are seldom angry for the reason we think. Mark and I were reacting to the symptoms not the deeper cause of our anger, which was neither of us had control over the fact that Mark was dying.

In *To See Differently*, a book about attitudinal healing, author Susan Trout tells how, when someone was negative toward her, she visualized the words as cannonballs of anger transforming into cotton puffballs. When Mark became caustic, I visualized his remarks as darts being thrown at me transforming into beautiful roses, slowly opening.

Eventually Mark wanted me do Reiki on him once again. I discovered that when I spent this hour each day connecting with him on a deeper level, we moved past all the surface aggravations, feeling our great love for one another again.

Anger still continued to rear its ugly head at times, however. One target was the amount of the medical bills, which often angered Mark. Once, he was convinced he had been billed for the bone scan he refused and he believed Dr. Anders had authorized it. I became angry at him for still being angry at Dr. Anders. Why couldn't he forgive him and let it go? I believe strongly that for healing to take place we need to forgive others. At the same time I could understand Mark's annoyance. I wished doctors were more aware of what they say and how they say it and what a powerful affect it has on the attitudes and healing of their patients.

In February 1993 when I went to a weekend retreat for educators at Virginia Beach, I realized how much I needed a break. I was rejuvenated by seeing old friends and the mental stimulation of new ideas, and I felt motivated to return to my work in education again. I'd become so isolated, living in the country with only Mark's illness on my mind. The ocean soothed my soul as well.

It is hard for me to ask for help. I go directly to God but don't share my feeling with others. When friends called to find out how I was doing, I put up a brave front, finding it difficult to express my emotions. One close friend from Michigan visited and wanted to know where I was emotionally. All I could say was, "I'm okay. I pray for Mark's highest good. I'm at peace with what is happening. I'm very sad about it, but what else could you expect after spending thirty-five years with my soul mate who is dying?" Except for my first eighteen years, I'd been with Mark my whole life.

My friend and I stayed overnight with a mutual friend and met other interesting, vibrant people, all actively involved in good causes. I felt a twinge—the world had gone on without me. We visited with Cozy Baker at her home and "oohed" and "aahed" at her newest additions to the world's largest collection of kaleidoscopes. For the next two days we took pictures with the kaleidoscope lens on my friend's camera. It was crazy and fun and just what I needed. I felt some "survivors's guilt" for having fun, but common sense told me I'd be more able to be present for Mark if I got away now and then. I suspected it was good for Mark to have a break from me, too.

Chapter Fifteen

Struggling Against Depression

In March, we returned to the doctor for the news that the tumors hadn't reduced in size. Mark was given two weeks off therapy to regain normalcy. I wondered what "normalcy" meant now with all the destruction going on inside Mark's body—destruction, yes, from cancer, but mostly from the treatments. Mark told Dr. Hawkins he was ready to check the Yellow Pages for Dr. Kervorkian's phone number unless Dr. Hawkins had a gun in his bottom drawer and just wanted to shoot him. Dr. Hawkins said, "Let's don't shoot you, let's shoot the interferon." We all laughed together. Mark decided to try gamma interferon three times a week for a month.

During that month of treatments, Mark fell into a depression. He didn't feel like doing anything. He was upset over financial matters and hospital bills; he felt sick and exhausted. I wavered, not knowing my own best course of action. Should I try to cheer him up or should I just listen and assure him it was okay to feel depressed? I tried to do both. We had planned on a trip south for a couple of weeks, but now he said he didn't care about anything.

When I felt depressed at the thought of losing him, I realized I was losing just one person. I imagined how he must feel to be losing everyone he loved. In doing this, I became amazed he wasn't more depressed. I was truly touched by his strength and courage.

After a month of gamma interferon there was no increase in the size of the tumors. He went off all treatment for the month of April to try to gain weight. He also got a supply of inhalers from a pulmonary specialist as it was often difficult for him to breath. Again, we used the reprieve from treatment to take a trip. This time we drove to Atlanta, dined at a favorite restaurant, and visited my niece and her family. We continued to New Orleans. By this time, Mark's spirits had returned to a higher level, but I noticed a big decline in his physical strength. Always before I could barely keep up with his long-legged stride; now I had to walk slowly, sometimes forgetting and getting ahead of him. He had to stop often to rest. Once in the hotel he could not get his breath. I quickly dug in my bag for the inhaler. He slowly regained normal breathing.

After we rested from that scary experience, we went downstairs and had a Manhattan, a drink we hadn't had in years. We treated ourselves to a rich French dinner and walked Bourbon Street. Unfortunately, the blues music pouring out into the street made me feel even more blue. We couldn't stay inside the bars because of the cigarette smoke.

Leaving New Orleans, we toured the alligator-filled bayou and plantations along the Mississippi River. We stayed overnight in a bed and breakfast created from small slave cabins. As we sat in rocking chairs on the front porch, sipping the complimentary wine, Mark turned to me, grinning, and said, "See, the slaves didn't have it so bad." He still enjoyed rattling my cage.

By May, the stress was taking its toll on our daughters too, especially Teresa. Emotions erupted over Memorial Day weekend. Teresa loved to immerse herself in dramatic productions and became very irritated if anyone talked during a show. We were watching a moving Memorial Day special on television, and Mark made some politically judgmental remarks, irritating Teresa. Relations for the rest of the evening were very strained. In the morning when she and I were alone, I said, "It's too bad you let your dad's remarks get to you." A floodgate of repressed anger opened—not just that Mark had spoiled the program by talking but that his negative remarks reminded her that she also tends to use sarcasm as a wrap for anger and putdowns and judgments as weapons. She didn't like this about herself and wanted to change.

Teresa, depressed over her dad's illness, couldn't tolerate feeling angry toward him. She left the house crying. My heart ached for all of us. When Mark found out that Teresa had left, he asked in a hurt voice, "She couldn't even wait two minutes to say goodby to me?"

He knew he had upset her. I tried to explain that she reacted to his quick sarcasm, recognizing her own tendency to do the same thing. I wanted him to see how his negativity affected all of us, but all he heard was that Teresa didn't want to be like him. The pain in his eyes engulfed me as well.

"Oh my God, what have I done?" I thought. Having unwittingly caused pain to two of the people I loved most in the world, I fled to the woods to a special tree I call my "listening post" to cry. My pain was as deep as anything I'd ever felt because I knew this relatively insignificant incident devastated Mark. My attempt to discuss issues openly had made things worse not better. Although I knew I hadn't created the schism, I was caught in the middle, trying to get them to understand one another.

When I finished crying, I went inside and asked Mark how he was feeling. "Totally empty," he said. I phoned Teresa and told her what I'd said and done. I told her she and Mark had to talk. Then I put Mark on the line. They talked and cried until they felt better. They agreed to meet the next day to talk some more. Teresa had decided to meet with Mark even before I called. Here is their reconciliation in her own words:

Mom put Dad on the phone and then the dam burst. All the fear and hurt I had been stuffing inside just spilled out. "I'm so afraid of losing you. It hurts to see you go through this. I'm so angry about all the things I know now we will never experience together." Everything just tumbled out—all the BAD stuff I had been holding onto because I was afraid Dad would feel bad about how upset I was. That opening gave him an opportunity to tell me all the things he had been holding back for fear of making me feel worse.

We had always done a good job of sharing our hope and love and faith, but out of our love and concern for each other we had held back on really sharing the other emotions like fear and pain and sadness. Without anywhere to go, those emotions had been creeping out in ways we did not mean to show it.

We decided to get together the next day and finish our talk in person. We spent the whole morning in my apartment talking about everything. He shared many things from and about his own life, his doubts, his fears. I saw many of my own feelings and struggles reflected in his.

And I really understood how special our bond was. We were so much alike that we served as mirrors for each other. Everything Dad was telling me he admired about me I admired most about him, but had difficulty seeing in myself.

I shared the things I was trying to change in myself and Dad acknowledged those same traits were ones he wished he could change, too.

What a rare thing to be able to share in the awareness of someone who is struggling with the same questions that you are but from the perspective of being on the verge of leaving this world. Many of the things Dad told me that day I had heard before, but they carried with them the power of truths acquired after much sacrifice.

I asked Dad if he had any regrets. "No," he said, "I really do not regret any of the decisions that I have made, but I do feel a sense of opportunities missed over not exploring some of the things I felt called to do."

I carry the memory of that day with me always, holding it close to my heart like a talisman. The exact things said that day may fade with time, but nothing can dim the memory of our lives bound together, sharing honestly from the heart all the things that we most needed to say.

To my relief, Mark came home exhilarated from that meeting with Teresa. He decided to set aside a time when he and Kristen could talk too. Here is their meeting, in Kristen's words:

When Dad used my nickname and said, "Hey, Bean, will you come and talk for a minute?" It really hit me. I knew this was it and I didn't feel ready. Dad started. He talked about how much he loved us all and how important we were to him. He told me that he didn't know what was going to happen, but no matter what, he'd always be there for me, even if it wasn't in the physical sense. I had no idea what to say or where to start, so I just started talking. It felt strange at first, because I knew Dad knew that I loved him. I guess it just really makes an impact when you talk about that love and what it means to you. We continued on. There was a lot of hugging, and a lot of tears.

If Dad had passed away without this conversation happening, I would have still known that he loved me and would be with me always. I wasn't prepared for the immense impact that such a conversation could carry. There is such a difference between knowing someone loves you and hearing it from them. Just a few short words opened up the road for such sharing

and expressing—it was incredible. I will carry that conversation with me for the rest of my life. I will always
have the comfort of knowing how much I meant to
Dad. I will also know that I was able to express to him
how much he meant to me.

Mark now realized his negativity had become habitual,
and he made an effort to break the pattern, improving the
atmosphere for all of us. The emotional purging cleared
the air and helped lift Mark's depression. After that, he
stayed in a much better, more positive mood.

In June, Mark felt well enough to join my sister Mayva
and her daughter and grandson for a few days in North
Carolina. Again I was startled to see how weak he had become. He could walk all right on level ground, but he had
to exert himself on even a mild incline. Tired by the day's
activities, he went to bed and fell into a deep sleep. He
woke me in the middle of the night with some choice exple-
tives. He had wet the bed. It was the beginning of the final
phase of losing control, the phase that also assaults one's
sense of personal dignity.

For Father's Day, the girls and I wanted to buy a couple
of kayaks so Mark and I could float on our river with little
effort. I thought the water and fresh air would be a good
tonic. Our big boat was for sale; it was too physically de-
manding to take it out. Mark said, "Thanks, but no thanks"
to the kayaks. He had no interest in any more boats of any
kind.

I bought myself one anyway and spent many quiet
moments of moving meditation on the river. As Mark became sicker, I found it harder to quiet my mind in
meditation. I still felt in constant dialogue with Spirit, especially as I floated on the river, silently chanting a song I'd
heard on a Coletta Long tape: "Oh my God, my God, how
I love thee, how I love thee, how I love thee." I chanted it
over and over, letting the words soothe, calm, and refresh
me. That kayak was one of the best purchases I'd ever made.

Teresa, Kristen, and I took Mark to Virginia Beach for Father's Day weekend. He was able to ride a bike on the flat boardwalk, and the ocean waves put us all in a relaxed mood. We played games and had good family fun. After that weekend Mark became very tired. He started sleeping a lot during the day.

On the Fourth of July, we watched the fireworks from the marina in downtown Washington, D.C. Our friends Gary and Dorien joined us. Mark and Gary talked about the pros and cons of early retirement. Mark certainly had no regrets about retiring early. If talking to a man dying of cancer could help someone else put things into perspective, then Mark was happy to help. I suspect very few dying men would say they wished they'd spent more time at the office.

By mid-July, Mark began coughing more, sometimes coughing up very large, bloody bronchial plugs. At first we didn't know what they were. Some looked like large worms. When the first large one came up, Mark said, "If it had moved, I'd have shot it." We saved it in a plastic bag in the freezer and took it with us to an appointment with a pulmonary specialist. The doctor was very impressed with the size, which in some weird way made Mark feel very satisfied. He excelled in bronchial plugs!

We had only just met this doctor, but on the return visit, he took Mark's hand in his and told him he really cared about him as a person. He had tears in his eyes. He said, "The scan of the lungs showed a very large tumor in a very bad place." Since we'd been tracking the tumors on X-ray every visit to the oncologist, we assumed he was talking about the same large tumors we already knew about. His level of concern reflected a deeply compassionate doctor, but we did not understand the true significance of what he as saying about the tumors.

At our next oncology appointment with Dr. Hawkins, we discovered he was referring to a large new tumor that had not been visible on X-rays. Our choices were narrowing: (1) Do nothing; (2) ICU; or (3) chemotherapy. Since varieties of interleukin-2 and interferon no longer seemed to be working, Dr. Hawkins suggested an experimental chemotherapy series that might shrink the tumors. If so, Mark would feel better and then could better stand the ICU treatment. The chemotherapy series would be done as a twenty-four hour infusion once a week on an outpatient basis. This could be done by installing a catheter under the skin in his neck. Always Dr. Hawkins held out hope. "If we get good results after four weeks, we can put alfa interferon and interleukin-2 on top of this." There was a new intern on duty that day, and Mark quipped to him, "We've still got the secret option—that's when Dr. Hawkins takes out a gun and shoots me." The regular nurses and doctors were used to Mark's joking, but the intern was visibly startled and didn't know how to respond.

After this appointment Mark went to the pulmonary department for a consultation. I stayed behind to get information on home health services because we wanted to take a trip to Minnesota in August and needed someone there to deliver the chemo and hook him up to it. Jane, our hospital liaison nurse, looked directly into my eyes and expressed her concern for the way things were headed. I started to cry. I could be strong until someone reached out to comfort me, then I fell apart. I nodded to Jane and went into the bathroom and cried racking, soundless sobs, so the woman in the next stall wouldn't hear me.

Mark was waiting when I emerged, and he knew by my eyes I'd been crying. He just winked and said, "What took you so long in there?" We passed the nurse who said, "I thought you'd already left." To which Mark responded flippantly, "No, we're having too much fun!" She replied, "Yes, this is a fun place all right!"

On the long ride home we were both quiet. We decided to find out if our insurance covered the ICU treatment. Mark had already made up his mind that he was not going to do it if it wasn't covered. This was the last ditch effort. The only reason to go the chemo route was to get him in better shape to be able to stand the ICU. He didn't want to take chemo and feel lousy if all it bought him was a couple more uncomfortable months.

When we got home, Mark went to bed. Neither of us wanted dinner. I went out on the river in my kayak and dangled my feet over the sides into the water. It was late July and the thermometer had registered a hundred degrees all day. Even now at seven in the evening, the water still felt like a warm bath with no difference in temperature between the air and the water. The sky was pink from the setting sun. I listened to the cheerful call of the bobwhite, the lonesome coo of the mourning dove, and the coarse croaking of a blue heron. In the distance a dog barked, and I thought of all the other families going about their normal daily routines. I felt very alone. I didn't paddle but just floated and prayed for divine wisdom to help me say, do, and be whatever would best serve Mark. I had a sudden intuitive feeling that Mark would die in November.

I remembered that Viktor Frankl survived the concentration camps by focusing on what he'd do and say about his experience when released. As I floated, I started to think about what I'd do in the future. I stopped myself because I didn't want to give energy to the thought of Mark's dying. I would just try to be present in each moment.

After much consideration, Mark decided to go for the chemo. He said he realized he was in a downward spiral and he needed to take charge again. He said, "Let's go for it and give it our best shot!" We went to the hospital and had the catheter put in just below his neck. The next day the home nurse came out to show me how to care for it, clean it, and change the bandages. When she asked Mark if the catheter bothered him when he moved, he said, "No, except when I play rugby."

My family had a reunion planned for August in Minnesota. Mark said he was going to make it there, "even if I have to crawl." Mark loved my family like his own, and I knew he wanted to see everyone one last time. We stopped at Mayva's in Minneapolis so we could get chemo delivered there before going to my tiny hometown of Herman.

The reunion at Herman was like a Norman Rockwell painting with more than fifty people, from my ninety-two-year-old mother to infants, chatting, playing, eating, and sharing at the local Odd Fellows Hall. We all enjoyed the opportunity to catch up with everyone else. We played softball by our own rules so everyone could play. Everyone had one pitch each inning, and the big kids had to bat left-handed. One-year-old Sam stood at the plate with his dad, "hit" the ball, and "ran" the bases in his dad's arms. Cameras clicked continuously throughout the day.

At our last dinner together three birthdays were celebrated, including Teresa's. The birthday cake decoration showed her skydiving, a feat she and Kristen accomplished before coming to the reunion. Mark was proud of their "daring do" spirit.

After dinner, my brother Bob asked for everyone's attention. "Mark wants to say a few words." I knew then that he was going to say goodbye. Mark stood up to address the group. He was emotional, choking on his words and holding his chest as he thanked my family for accepting him into the fold, ". . . even though I took the baby of the family away from you when she was only eighteen years old." His speech was really a testimony. He wanted my family to know how much he loved me and how much I had helped him— that he could not have done it without me. He expressed how lucky he was to have such wonderful daughters and how much they meant to him. In conclusion, he told my family, "I love you all very much."

Mark's voice wavered as he struggled to talk without crying, and I couldn't look at him because then I would cry and not be able to stop. Almost everyone else had tears in their eyes too. Teresa had our camcorder on as he began his remarks but the batteries went dead right after the first couple of sentences. Perhaps it was not meant to be on tape.

When he finished, there was silence. Mayva broke the tension with humor, "If the family could accept my husband, a wild Armenian, then a Norwegian was easy to accept!" A few more light comments and it was over. Everyone milled about the room.

Mayva's husband, Paul, was pacing out in the kitchen, wiping his eyes and saying, "Shit! It's not fair." His son-in-law was wiping his eyes too and said, "That really took a lot of courage to do." My family members love each other but we aren't accustomed to expressing our love out loud. My sister, Marian, had written a letter to tell Mark she loved him, and I heard Mark thank her for it. She said, "Well, we really do love you," and I figured that was some kind of a breakthrough for her.

Later that night Mark and my sister Darlene had a good long talk. I was in a sleeping bag on a pad on the floor, and she came in and hugged me, tears streaming down her cheeks. "I feel so bad about losing Mark."

So much love permeated our family gathering, it was an emotional overload for me. Besides Mark's farewell, I felt concern for Mother who looked more frail than the last time I had seen her. My brother Dick, too, looked wan from a recent heart attack. I had worried about Mark catching a cold or flu at the reunion, especially with so many little kids around. Mark's immune system couldn't stand much more stress. No one else had a cold, but I came down with one! I slept in a different room from Mark, bought face masks to wear and changed them every hour, and washed my hands constantly. He still caught my cold. He laughed. "See? I even brought my own 'Typhoid Mary' with me!"

Back in Minneapolis the nurse sent us to the emergency room for a blood transfusion because Mark's hemoglobin was down. We waited two hours and fifteen minutes before we saw the doctor, one hour for lab work to be done and then four hours for the transfusion. If you can still walk and aren't bleeding profusely, don't bother to go to a hospital emergency room for quick service.

Chapter Sixteen

Dreams and Remembrances

For years I have kept a dream journal. Mark did not but in the last few months of his life, his dreams became very vivid and we'd discuss them. In one dream he personally had to stop a deadly virus that was killing off everyone. He awoke, told me about it, then went back to sleep—and had the same dream. In the morning he reported, "It got me."

In another dream he was in a beautiful field, a very blissful, peaceful place like the meadow of his near-death experience. Someone was with him and at first he felt it was Mayva, but then he thought maybe it was my sister Phyllis who is in spirit. He awoke confused and disoriented not realizing for awhile he was in our bedroom. We agreed that most likely he was visiting in the spirit world at night. The next evening he wondered, "Will I go back to the other side again?"

He also dreamed about being in the military, perhaps consistent with his warrior essence and his current life-death struggle. In one dream he signed up for three more years in the Marines and wondered how he physically could do that. Then in his dream he said happily, "Hey! Wait a minute! I have cancer. I don't have to do that!"

Mark also had a whole series of dreams that were a sort of review of his life. After one such dream we both were wide awake at two in the morning and talked until dawn. He told me about some of the crazy things he had done as a teenager. Once he had improvised water skis by rounding off two boards and nailing rubber overshoes in the middle. He and his buddies spent a whole day laughing, drinking, and trying to get up on these "skis" pulled by a boat that had only a twenty-five horsepower motor.

We reminisced about how we met and what we did on our dates and how we felt about each other at first. He said, "I knew on our first date you were the right one for me."

I told Mark I had suspected married life with him was going to be interesting when, for our honeymoon, he took me on a four-week camping trip, from Minnesota south to Mexico and then north up the West Coast all the way to Seattle. And we didn't even have a tent! Just a tarp. We slammed the edge of the tarp into the door of our orange Volkswagen Bug and then staked the other ends out on the ground, forming a "roof" over two camp cots. Often we'd drive until late at night and pull off somewhere in the dark, awakening in the mornings to find curious cows gazing at us from a few feet away. Another great view from the honeymoon suite!

We remembered how on the way, we stopped in Las Vegas for a couple of days to "try our luck." Hot, dusty, and bedraggled from camping, Mark decided to clean his tennis shoes by wearing them into the shower. He squished squashed down the sidewalk, leaving big, wet, size-thirteen footprints. While we consumed the free food and drinks, we parlayed our initial gambling investment of five dollars into enough money to pay for our hotel and come out twelve dollars ahead. This was significant since we only had three hundred dollars to our name.

Settled as students in Seattle, we were poor, but so in love we didn't care. We laughed as we recalled some of the silly things we did. Walking on the beach one day at Vashon Island, Mark challenged me, "Bet you don't dare to walk into the water with your shoes on."

"Ha!" I threw down the gauntlet. "I can walk out further than you can." I waded up to my ankles. The icy bite of cold water did not deter us and when Mark waded past me up to his knees, I quickly waded out up to my thighs. Neither of us would concede. Fully clothed, we were soon in water up to our waists. Dripping wet but laughing and hugging, we rode the ferry back to Seattle.

The water around Seattle was too cold to swim in for very long so we made ourselves wet suits, gluing together thick rubber material. Then we bought secondhand weights and were ready to skin dive. In 1959, it was inexpensive to rent air tanks and no one bothered to ask us if we knew how to use them. Mark said, "We can figure it out. How complicated can it be?" We learned by doing and discovered several feet down a magnificent swaying kelp bed, abundant with many species of sea life. No wonder! Later we learned this was the spot where the city sewage was being discharged.

As we continued to review our early years together, water sports was a constant theme. Mark's brother-in-law had a collapsible kayak we would paddle along the waterfront shipyards, feeling tiny next to the large ocean-going vessels. Sometimes we played tag, running across the large log booms on Puget Sound, laughing as the big logs spun under our feet. Or we'd go camping by the ocean on an Indian reservation.

Once we had only enough money to buy food or to go to the beach camping with friends. Of course, we chose to go to the beach. All we had left to eat before the next paycheck, a week away, were a few potatoes, onions, and milk. I had a plan. "We'll dig for clams and I can make enough clam chowder for us to eat the rest of the week." It worked. We had a grand time and when we got home, I soon had a steaming pot of chowder cooking on the stove. It was delicious but needed just a little more salt. I shook the large salt shaker over the pot and the lid fell off, cascading an entire cupful of salt into our lovely chowder! Mark came into the kitchen as I shrieked, a look of dismay on his face when he saw me frozen in place, holding the empty shaker over the pot. Once over the initial shock, we howled with laughter. I had just ruined the last of our food. But we were not defeated—we still had water. And we remembered that we had a reserve supply of dehydrated camp food. We dug it out and feasted on scrambled eggs.

So many memories. It was very satisfying to reminisce together. As we lay holding hands, the morning light began to stream across our bed, and we felt content.

We spent August 23, our thirty-fifth anniversary, at Virginia Beach in an old hotel that had a veranda with rocking chairs so he could sit comfortably and still be on the beach. He was so thin then, down to 150 pounds. I had to pad his chair with pillows. Mark was analytical about his thinness. "Did you know, Joany, that you can always tell when someone is about to die because their teeth look too big for their head?" He added, "So now, every morning I look in the mirror and smile!" It was true. I had been noticing his teeth more.

As we rocked and watched the ocean waves, I pondered the process of Mark's adventurous spirit moving from flying his beloved airplane to rocking on the veranda. I remembered a time we flew from Washington, D.C., to Topeka, Kansas. Teresa and Kristen, aged five and seven, were playing quietly, happily ensconced in the backseat of the small Cessna. We had charted our journey and planned to refuel after flying over the mountains. But the fog was so thick that when Mark dropped altitude to see if we could break out of it, we could see the tops of trees but not the ground. Mark quickly nosed the plane back up, and since I was navigating, asked me to locate an alternate airport. I found one ninety miles away but our gas tanks were close to empty. We would never make it that distance. We had no choice. When Mark dropped back down we miraculously saw a river. Knowing the airport was somewhere close to it, he followed the river. By now the needles indicated that both of our tanks were empty.

Mark said calmly, "Joan, you'd better start praying. We need to look for a field where we can make an emergency landing." Then suddenly he throttled down to go in. Thankfully, he had finally spotted the airport and we landed safely. When we fueled the plane, we learned that the tanks had only two gallons of gas left, which meant only a couple more minutes of flying time. Teresa and Kristen had not even realized there was a crisis and were out skipping around, stretching their cramped legs. Kristen brought me a handful of dandelions. No flowers were ever more beautiful. My legs, on the other hand, were Jell-O. If I hadn't had to go to the bathroom so bad, I'm sure I wouldn't have been able to walk. Mark grinned and all he said was, "There is nothing to fear but fear itself."

I did not want to get back in that plane for the next leg of the journey but facing fear once was not enough for this trip. As I navigated, I needed to spot landmarks to make sure we were on course. Many times on that trip clouds obscured our vision; and when I couldn't stand flying blind any longer, I told God exactly what landmark I needed to spot below us. Magically the clouds would part, and I'd catch a quick glimpse of just that landmark before the clouds rolled back in, obscuring my view once again. This happened so often it strengthened my belief in spiritual guidance.

Now as we rocked and watched children play on the beach, I mulled over how we were flying blind again—this time on an uncharted journey. Flying blind but still being guided. And once more, Mark was showing me how to face my fears.

Back home, Bonnie and Rodney, who recently had also celebrated their thirty-fifth anniversary, brought out a long-saved bottle of 1975 Cuvee Dom Perignon to help us celebrate. "We can't think of a better occasion than this to share it with you, as we've been friends for over twenty years."

Later that night we showed slides of our five children growing up together and all the fun neighborhood celebrations. We laughed about how, when Mark had told Rodney, back in 1972, that we were going to put in a pool, the two of them decided, "Hey, we can put it in ourselves. After all, what is a pool but a big hole in the ground?" That was so typical of Mark's can-do spirit. A few weeks later, I stared down into a huge, gaping hole he had just dug in the back-yard with a borrowed back-hoe and wondered if he were really going to be able to pull this one off. The slides of our children playing in the beautiful twenty-four-foot by forty-eight-foot pool attested that he had. It was a neighborhood hit!

By the end of August Mark's condition showed no improvement from chemo. It was decided to continue but to consider taxol next, a chemical derived from the yew tree. Dr. Hawkins always suggested a new possible treatment to consider. A way of holding out hope, I guess.

That night, after a day at the hospital for appointments and CAT scan, Mark dreamed what he called a "massive dream." He woke up, went back to sleep, and went right back into the same dream. He was organizing and directing all the people on the planet on their way to heaven. Waves of people! My family came together as a group and asked him if we should wait for him and he said, "No, I have to finish my job first."

Perhaps I'd reached the acceptance stage in death and dying, for as painful as the process was, I somehow felt at peace with it now. If, after everything we'd tried—all the alternatives as well as Western medicine—Mark still was not going to be cured, then perhaps it was his time to go home to Spirit. We talked at length with Merrill and Jean about why some people are physically healed and others are not. I was uncomfortable with the term "exceptional patients" used for cancer survivors, because it implied Mark was "nonexceptional" if he didn't survive. I do not believe we die until our soul gives permission, so I trusted Mark's soul knew what it was doing. I continued to pray for his highest good knowing if that meant parting on this level we'd always be connected on the soul level.

Dorien sent Mark a lovely reading she'd received from her spirit guides. They called Mark "Master." They went on to say, "You are a powerful warrior spirit. Your strength, honor, and conviction to high principles are recognized in both dimensions. Many are those, in both dimensions, who count themselves blessed to be your friend or of your family. We know you too, beloved, and are also grateful to be so counted."

Teresa wrote of the changes she was seeing:

From the time Dad returned from the trip to Herman I started to really notice the changes in him. My employers were incredibly supportive, and I was able to take days off to go and be with him.

Once Mom had asked me to come out on a Friday and stay with Dad because she had a workshop to present. Dad was sleeping a lot by this time, so I brought a stack of books and sat by the side of the bed while he slept. Every now and then, he would rouse a bit, squeeze my hand, and say, "I love you," and we'd talk awhile before he would drift back off to sleep.

During one of our conversations he said, "So work is getting to you?" I realized he was referring to my need to take a day off. I said, "No, not so much." He immediately responded, "Oh, no, did you take the day off just to watch me?" I heard the pain in his knowing that he had reached the stage where he had to have someone there to take care of him.

When he fell back asleep I went out in the woods to cry. It hurt so much and I didn't think it would ever be okay again. I sat in the woods and asked God for a sign that things were going to work out—that if I saw a deer that would be an omen. So I sat and waited and waited, and my sign never came. Feeling completely alone, I went back inside.

Since Dad had not been eating much, I decided to go to the store to see if I could come up with something that would tempt his appetite. On the way back from the store I passed our neighbors' driveway. Perched there just on the entrance to the driveway was one of those plastic deer, posing with one leg raised. I stopped because I could not remember having seen this lawn ornament before. That's when I noticed that the plastic deer was breathing. I sat there for the longest time just watching that deer. We were about three feet apart, facing each other. Finally, it dropped its foot and dashed away into the woods.

God had sent me my sign, but in his own time rather than mine. I wondered how many other signs I had missed because I was only looking for them on my terms.

I fixed some enchiladas for dinner. Dad had always loved spicy food, the hotter the better! I knew that he could no longer tolerate the really spicy stuff, so I got mild chiles for the enchiladas. He took a few bites and then had to pick the chiles out because even the mild ones were too much for him. So many things were changing, but it was these little physical things that really brought it home to me.

One warm day, I sat on the back deck thinking about all the changes in our life since Mark had gotten cancer. Bird songs enhanced my reverie. Suddenly I heard the roar of a chain saw coming from the lot next to ours.

"Oh no, construction sounds in my woods!" The tree I claimed as my listening post would no longer be there for me. Its lovely tree trunk dipped just enough to create a place to sit and lean back on before it soared boldly toward the sky. When I sat there in an attitude of inner quietness, a reassuring power seeped into me. I felt a great sadness as chain saws ripped through the trees and I heard them fall, one by one. I knew the young couple who were building and they also loved the land and river. Soon their three-year-old son would be playing in the woods, learning to love nature, just as I had as a child. Life goes on; we learn and grow from all experiences and from the changes we meet along our path. Nothing ever stays the same.

Chapter Seventeen

Countdown to Eternity

In early September, Mark's two sisters and brother-in-law flew from Seattle for a visit. It was bittersweet because we all knew it was probably the last. They joined us for a typical day at Gerogetown Hospital for a doctor's appointment and then a hearing test. Mark's hearing had grown steadily worse and his ears were plugged up. The doctor wanted to be sure that he did not have an infection of the inner ear that would jeopardize his immune system even more.

September 10 marked the birthday of Mark's father, who had died just a couple years before at the age of 103. Since his sisters and brother-in-law were going home that day, we planned to have lunch before I took them to the airport. After the blessing, his brother-in-law expressed his love for Mark, telling him he'd never known a more courageous man and that he'd met lots of them. Mark's sisters both added a few words although they were too emotional to say all they wanted to say.

Mark was visibly moved but when he started to talk, gibberish came out of his mouth instead. Then he started to choke, whooping, and gasping for breath. I jumped up to rub a certain spot on his back, which a friend had shown me would help stop his coughing spasms. The three others began to pray. I thought, "Oh no, he's going to die on his father's birthday!"

It seemed forever before Mark could get his breath. We were all very shaken but I sat down, and we passed food around while Mark rested his head in his hands. He tried to speak and had another choking spasm. Again I didn't know if he'd make it and thought, "Oh please, don't have him go this way."

When he pulled out of that one, I walked him to bed and continued to rub his back. No one felt like eating and they put the food away. Not wanting to leave Mark in this state, I asked our neighbor to take the family to the airport. They slipped away quietly. No more lengthy goodbyes, as it literally made Mark choke on his words. It was very difficult for all of us.

Saturday I busied myself cleaning house, and on Sunday Teresa and Kristen came out and provided support. We did a lot of crying, mostly when we were alone, as reflected in Kristen's writing:

> Sometimes I'd just cry, and sometimes I'd try to hold the tears back because I was so tired of crying. One night in particular I remember. Mom and Dad were in their bedroom and I was sleeping on the floor in the living room. I heard Dad try to say something. His voice was choked and his breathing was labored, but I could distinctly hear what he said: "Joan, if I get to be too much trouble, you let me know." I lost it. Everything seemed to hit me at once, and I just sobbed into my pillow.

Sunday night after Teresa and Kristen left and the house was quiet, I had a long cry on the couch. When Mark would start to cough, I'd go back in with him. I found it hard to sleep next to him while he was struggling to breathe. I couldn't imagine slowly being smothered and thought if he couldn't be healed, I hoped he could go quickly and quietly in his sleep.

Monday morning I was still feeling weepy at the breakfast table watching him struggle to eat. That made Mark emotional and as he tried to say comforting words to me, he choked up and a spasm almost started again. We realized we had to snap out of this and not let ourselves get emotional. He regained control, and we became almost businesslike.

That night he continually dreamed of attempting a frustrating, very precise job in which he had to take exactly ten cells out and peel them. Each time, he failed and had to do it all over. The cells were shaped like a T (healthy T cells are needed to fight cancer). Although he awoke several times, whenever he fell asleep the same dream picked up right where it had left off. I wondered if medically there was some cancer cure clue or significance for peeling ten T cells.

By the end of September, I couldn't imagine how time could go so slowly and so fast at the same time. Each day Mark became weaker. After showering, he'd be so exhausted from the exertion that he needed me to dry him off. He'd rest again before getting dressed. Some days he just stayed in bed.

October brought pretty fall days, sunny but chilly at night. As I gazed at the harvest moon, I wondered how much longer before Mark could go home to Spirit. I felt the end of his life approaching much like the cycle of nature with the leaves floating from the trees, knowing spring would follow. Teresa called one morning to say Mark had come to her in her dream saying goodbye because he was off to fight a war. It was so real, she called, almost expecting him to be gone.

It felt unnatural to give up feeding him, but I finally stopped trying to entice him to eat. If he thought of something that might taste good, I'd run to the store and get it. Usually all he could eat would be a couple of bites. Cream of Wheat became a staple. But I still pushed fluids so he wouldn't become dehydrated; he could drink chocolate Ensure if I heated it.

We now made weekly visits to the hospital where they hooked him up to an IV for more fluids. Dr. Hawkins put Mark on hormones to see if it would stimulate his appetite. Next to us in the room an elderly man was getting a blood transfusion, and I heard myself echoed in his wife's ministrations. "Do you want more to drink?"

"No," he said.

"But you are supposed to drink more."

"I don't care!"

I heard the desperation and exhaustion in her voice. She had one other job I didn't have—helping him with the urinal every couple of minutes. She was old and tired and sad; my heart went out to her.

By now, Mark's weight was down to 134 pounds; driving the hour and a half into the Georgetown hospital became too tiring for him. During our last visit to the hospital none of the doctors suggested any more treatments, but even then, Dr. Hawkins and Dr. Wojtowicz assured Mark they would be there for him. The home nurse would visit once a week and take blood work so they could monitor him. They prescribed decongestant pills and said they could order oxygen if Mark wanted it.

In private, I asked Dr. Wojtowicz what to expect, specifically how Mark might die. Dr. Wojtowicz was caring as he listed the possibilities. He could choke on a bronchial plug. Blood clots could form in the legs or pelvis. If the calcium level in his blood rose higher, there would be slow dehydration and he could die in his sleep. Or he could just waste away.

As we were leaving, Mark shook hands with them, expressing his gratitude to them. They were deeply touched. For the last time, I wheeled him out of the Lombardi Cancer Center. Mark did not want to die in a hospital, and I didn't want that either.

Once at home I learned how to hook him up to the IV fluids to keep him feeling as comfortable as possible. Now I too was running with the urinal about every hour. At first, Mark tried to reach for it himself, but after he spilled it once, I tried to anticipate when he would need it.

Mark began to lose his hair. After taping plastic wrap over his catheter, just as I did before he showered, I helped him into the tub to wash his hair. Clumps of his baby soft hair came out, sticking to my fingers. The bath felt good to him and it was less tiring than standing up in the shower. The bottom of the tub, when I drained it, was a mat of hair.

I began to notice that Mark was picking up my thoughts—or was I picking up his? I might be thinking of a song and he'd start to sing it. Early one morning, lying in bed, I was thinking the odd thought that bacon and eggs cooked in the grease might taste good to him. I had not cooked bacon in over three years. He woke up and said, "Maybe I could eat some bacon and greasy eggs."

This telepathic communication happened often. An even more unusual thing happened one evening as I was sitting on the couch in the great room. I had avoided thinking about plans for Mark's memorial service, but perhaps I needed to start facing it. Feeling very sad, I was thinking about what kind of a tribute I might give.

Suddenly I heard a rattling that became quite loud. I looking around the room to see where the noise was coming from. Startled, I realized a painting was rattling against the wall! I could see absolutely no logical reason for it to rattle. There was no breeze. The air vent was not blowing but the painting was bouncing back and forth against the wall. None of the numerous other paintings jumped around. Then I realized it was a print that Mark's sister had given us many years ago in Seattle. I thought maybe it was time to call them to let them know the end was near. Next I felt an urgent need to go check on Mark. When I went into the bedroom, I found him crying. I knelt beside the bed and gathered him into my arms. He said, "We can do this. We'll do it together, one day at a time." I gave him my tribute then. "I love you so much. You have taught me how to live life without fear." He whispered back, "You taught me how to love."

I don't understand what made the picture rattle on the wall. Maybe Mark picked up on my thinking of his memorial. Maybe it was his thoughts or energy from an emotionally charged atmosphere. Maybe angels were letting me know he needed me at that moment. Whatever caused it, the picture stopped rattling when I went to him. I decided not to think about his memorial anymore.

At other times Mark commented on his death as a detached observer. He said, "It really is an interesting process," and he wondered what the next stage would be and what that would be like. When I was sad, he'd hold me in his arms and say, "Don't cry, it's not so bad." Then he'd say, "Whatever is, is."

He told me what songs he wanted at his memorial service. Teresa had sung *Amazing Grace* at his father's funeral, and he wanted her to sing it again for him. I told him I'd talk with her about it. I figured the only way she could do that would be to tape it.

Several years ago I gave Mark a tape by the Don Cossack Singers. He had been visibly moved by the song *Bright and Clear Tolls the Little Bell*, and said he wanted it played at his funeral, even though we had no idea what the Russian words to the song meant. He reminded me of that now. He also wanted *Rock of Ages* to be played and the serviced closed with *Taps*.

Mark wanted to make a tape himself to be played at his memorial. He said he had his opening line ready, "As unaccustomed as I am to speaking at my own funeral . . . ." I discouraged him as I was afraid he might choke up and go into another spasm trying to do that. It would be very hard for me to listen to his labored breathing and swollen tongue speech, and I thought it would be painful for others as well. Maybe I was wrong and should have encouraged him. We had made a point of saying and doing everything we wanted to so that we would have no regrets later. However, I do have regrets over this.

Two nights in a row Mark dreamed that people in black were delivering soot to cover the whole world, and he was trying to stop them.

Another time he said he had a vision. "I don't know if it was a dream or not. I don't think I was asleep and it somehow seemed different from a dream." A large black slab fell in front of him and two beings in black said, "You can go on or you can stay here and be totally healed." He chose to stay as there were three things he wanted to do yet. I asked him what they were and he said, "I want to walk our daughters down the aisle." I couldn't say anything. I just sat there until I knew my voice would not tremble. Then I asked what the other two were, and he softly and sadly whispered, "I don't know. I can't remember." We sat quietly for a minute, and then he added, "It really would be a miracle that no one could deny if I were to be healed now." Mark accepted his death, yet even in the final stage of dying, the acceptance stage, I believe one can still hope for a miracle.

During the day I often found it difficult to understand his speech, but at night he talked very loudly and clearly in his sleep and carried on extraordinarily technical and intelligent conversations, using words I never knew were in his vocabulary. He used words I had never heard before and even complicated chemical formulas.

I can't tell you exactly what it was, but I knew when there was a shift—that Mark was releasing his hold on life and was really getting ready now to make his transition. We were visiting with friends who had stopped in with soup they had made for Mark. I saw a change in Mark's eyes. He smiled slightly as he appeared to follow the conversation, sometimes even commenting, but mostly he just smiled with a faraway look in his eyes. He wasn't totally present. I think he was half here and half in spirit.

In mid-October I was scheduled to teach a class at the local college. I canceled it. Our home nurse said she didn't think he'd make it through the weekend. His heartbeat was wildly erratic. I called Mark's sister, Dussie. She and her husband Ran arrived the next day. Teresa and Kristen were already with us.

Mark didn't die that weekend. The girls took some days off. When they did go back to work, they drove out again in mid-week. "It's hard to drive," said Kristen, "when you're crying the whole way."

It is also hard to maintain your dignity when you get to the point of not being able to manage elimination needs, certainly the last thing one wants to lose control over. Once before, after he started treatment, Mark had to go to the hospital emergency room with an impacted bowel. I didn't want that to happen again. I became concerned when he was constipated and after consulting the doctor gave him an enema. When that didn't work I gave him a suppository. I put adult diapers on him as he could no longer move fast enough to get to the bathroom in time. That night I changed him eight times. He never complained once.

A few days later Mark was constipated again, although he had hardly eaten anything. He wanted to use the commode. Dussie helped me get him into the bathroom. With his arms over our shoulders, we carried his frail body slowly, step by step. It was all he could do to sit on the commode, and he was tiring fast. When I started to wipe him, I felt the hard stool protruding partially expelled. As gently as I could, I physically manipulated the stool out. I'm sure this caused physical discomfort and suspect the psychological pain was even greater. I thought, "Oh, Mark, my love, did you ever think it would come to this?" He withstood this latest indignity with such grace. That was Mark's last trip to the bathroom.

Most of the day I would sit on the bed and hold my hand on Mark's forehead and on his back. We didn't talk. The words had all been spoken. I wanted Mark to know he was never alone, so I'd get under the covers of the bed with him and sit so he could always feel my body. Except to go to the bathroom, I didn't leave his side, until nine or ten at night. Then Ran and Dussie would sit with him and I'd take my walk, a time to release the pent up emotions.

On these walks, I cried aloud like a wounded animal so by the time I reached the river I could be still and let the energy flow back into my depleted soul. As I walked to the river, the moon reflected off the sandy path just enough to allow me to walk safely. I never took a flashlight as I wanted nothing to interfere with the velvet darkness. One overcast night no light glimmered from the sky, only utter blackness. Suddenly I was scratched and snagged by branches and bushes. Thinking I was following the path, I had failed to make a curve and been pitched into the brambles. How like life! But we can self-correct; utter darkness is only the absence of light.

Friends and neighbors brought in food. One neighbor brought in enough sandwich fixings for lunches to last a week. Another friend who taught all day still found time to bring over a vegetarian meal almost every night. I fed Mark Cream of Wheat slowly, spoonful by spoonful, wiping the corners of his mouth with the spoon to catch any drips, just as I had fed our children as babies.

Ran and Dussie went to the store to get anything that was needed, served the food, did dishes, and everything else around the house. I don't know how I could have gotten through it without their help. Dussie is a nurse, which gave me great comfort we were doing everything we could. Ran desperately wanted to help so I didn't hesitate to ask him to run errands. When Mark developed a nasty bed sore, Ran fashioned a foam pad with a hole cut out for Mark's hip.

Thirty-five years ago we had begun our married life with Ran and Dussie when we lived in the apartment above their house in Seattle while we finished college. Now they were here for us at the end.

Chapter Eighteen

The Sacred Vigil

Thursday, October 29

Mark asked for a White Castle hamburger. We do not have the White Castle chain out here in Virginia. As a boy in Minnesota, Mark would get a quarter from his mother and go downtown for three White Castle hamburgers, a pot of beans, and chocolate milk. Mark and his friends used to order the number of hamburgers by holding up the number on their fingers and then point to their armpits. The boyhood joke was that was how they flattened the patties. One of our rituals every year when we'd go to Minnesota to visit family was to go for burgers at White Castle.

Earlier, when I was racking my brain to find something he'd like to eat, I had checked all the grocery stores for frozen White Castle hamburgers and I couldn't find any. So I didn't hold out much hope when Dussie took off to the store to see if she could find some. I couldn't believe it when she returned with a box of them from our closest store. They had not been there when I had looked, and I've never seen them there since. Can a miracle look like a White Castle hamburger?

Mark ate the whole hamburger and enjoyed it thoroughly. Intuitively I knew that was the last food he would eat. Somehow it seemed appropriate.

More friends flooded in with flowers and food. It was enough for them just to sit by the side of the bed and hold Mark's hand. Some were more comfortable doing that than others. Much of the time I felt Mark was more in spirit than here. When friends and family sat down beside him, he'd squeeze their hand, greet them by name, and whisper a word or two. Then he seemed to drift off somewhere. Those who were able to sit silently just holding his hand received the blessing of witnessing death in its peaceful final stages.

Rodney could not sit still very long with his dying friend. When he left for the last time he bent over and whispered in Mark's ear, "Goodbye, buddy. Save me a seat up front."

Saturday, several friends, Teresa, Kristen, and I were all sitting on or near the bed talking, reminiscing, and telling "I remember when Mark . . ." stories. We laughed and cried together. We were there with Mark, but he was no longer really with us. He had detached and just lay quietly.

A kitten appeared on our deck right off the bedroom. We didn't feed it for the first day hoping it would return to its owners. But it sat outside the sliding glass door and watched us, pressing its face and paws against the glass, meowing softly. Finally, Kristen couldn't stand it any longer and put out food and made it a warm bed. Purring, it snuggled into our arms and gave us such a feeling of love and comfort. Because of Kristen's allergies, we didn't invite it into the house. The kitten stayed for a few days and then as suddenly as it had appeared, it disappeared. A friend listened intently as I told her this story and then said, "Joan, we have an old Scottish legend that just before someone is to die, a cat will appear."

Sunday, October 31—Halloween

At five in the morning Mark had a very hard time breathing and asked me to get him oxygen. He had not wanted it before. I called our home nurse to order it. Since it could take hours for it to be delivered, I called 911. I told them Mark didn't want to be rushed to the hospital, but he needed help in the interim. They agreed to honor his wishes and brought oxygen within a short time. Once hooked up to oxygen they were going to give him a shot of morphine to relax him and help him breathe more easily. Mark must have been concerned about where the rescue squad person was going to give that first shot of morphine, and he clutched his leg and said something like "squish." It was difficult for him to talk because of all the mucus in his throat so I asked him a couple of times to repeat what he was trying to tell us. Finally with a look of exasperation, he spelled it out f-l-e-s-h and pinched his inner thigh to show us there was still a little bit of flesh there where they could get the needle in to give the shot. We were all relieved they could give the shot through the catheter instead.

Monday, November 1

Even with the "swish and swallow" mouth rinse the doctors prescribed, Mark's lips and mouth became very sore, caked, and cracked with smelly ulcers. Thick sticky mucus kept coming up and rattled in his throat. I got up several times during the night to clear it. I tried Q-tips but they were too small. Finally I wrapped my finger with gauze and stuck it in his mouth to swab the mucus out. The next morning I ordered a suction pump, which helped a great deal.

It was a dilemma. Should we keep him on fluids or not? If it kept him more comfortable—yes. If it prolonged his life and he became too weak to cough up bronchial plugs—no. The bed sore on his hip was getting worse also. If we removed fluids, would he die faster? I decided there was a chance fluids made him feel more comfortable, so I kept him hooked to the IV. My love for him was great enough to want to free him, but I didn't want him to suffer. I slept only a couple hours a night and was so tired I couldn't think straight. All I could do was to pray we were doing what was best for him.

At times I even wondered if my almost constant presence prevented him leaving. I wasn't hanging on any more, but I wanted to stay vigilant to assist him however I could in his spiritual transition. It seemed that spiritual helpers were gathered around him. Once he said there was a third person in the bathroom and I just nodded. I didn't want to question him further in his weakened state. Another time when we were alone, he told me the room was full of people. I believe there is a veil that separates physical and spiritual dimensions, and it was now lifting for Mark.

Other times Mark would hold his arms out wide, as though he were embracing the world. Then he'd fold his hands and stretch them out again, palm side up. He would do this over and over. Whatever it meant, it was a beautiful ritual. He'd also say "okay, okay" many times during his sleep, and I wondered if he were getting instructions from the spiritual dimension. I remember my sister Phyllis also had said "okay" a lot as she was dying.

Because I was looking for signs, I was a bit too quick to assign a metaphysical meaning to everything. Once he whispered to me he wanted to be on the other side. So I tenderly and lovingly assured him it was all right for him to leave. I told him to look toward the light, that there would be spiritual beings there to help him. He repeated two more times that he wanted to be on the other side, and I continued to lovingly reassure him it was all right for him to leave. Finally, with a look of resignation, he began to heave himself over, as best as he could, so that he could lie on his other side. I felt very silly as I helped him roll over to the other side and I had to laugh at myself.

Wednesday, November 3

In the late afternoon Mark became very determined and told us he was leaving. I was more cautious now attributing meaning to what he said. He told us he wanted his billfold, which we got for him. Then he wanted his watch on and extended his arm upward. I put it on and clasped it but it fell down right up to his elbow because he was so thin. Then he wanted to put his clothes on. Dussie and I helped him put on a T-shirt, took off the diapers, and put on a pair of jockey shorts. Next he wanted to sit up, so we helped him sit on the edge of the bed. He definitely thought he was going somewhere and he wanted to do it on his own. Weakly, he pushed us both aside with his arms and then struggled to stand up. Of course, he could not muster the strength and realizing this, he wearily laid back down and closed his eyes.

He usually choked when drinking fluids through a straw, but he continued to ask for sips of water. Dussie didn't want to be the one to give it to him anymore as she was afraid he would aspirate liquid into his lungs. So if he wanted water when she was there, she would ask me to hold the glass for him.

Wednesday evening Mark took a sip of water and began to cough. I don't know if he aspirated or not but later, in the middle of the night, I could hear a change in the rattle in his breathing. I woke Dussie and Ran. Because Dussie is hard of hearing, she could not hear the difference but she settled into the lounge chair we'd brought into the bedroom. It was two o'clock and I'd given him a morphine shot to relax his breathing. I was going to give him another shot at five if he needed it. As I sat next to Mark in bed, I rolled a little brass ball around slowly on my palm. The soft gentle chimes inside the ball made a very soothing sound.

I guess I must have dozed off. I was awakened suddenly by the smell of urine and immediately got up to run the tapwater so it would get warm, got a diaper, and started to clean and change Mark. He had voided and unfortunately I had forgotten to put diapers back on him after we'd changed him into shorts earlier when he said he was leaving. Dussie awoke from the chair and started to help me. Mark was warm, and as I struggled to get his arm out of his wet shirt, I said, "He is really sound asleep." His arm flopped heavily back down on the bed. Suddenly I noticed there was no rattle. In that same moment, the realization struck Dussie too and she said, "He's gone." I thought I had heard him breathing when I got up, but I was so busy getting him out of his wet underwear that I failed to notice he was breathing his last breath. He died peacefully in his sleep. Dussie kept saying, "Thank you, Jesus," as she helped me finish changing the sheets and then left the room.

Thursday, November 4, 1993, 6:30 a.m.

I cradled Mark's head in my arms and cried louder and longer than I have ever cried in my whole life. I collected myself long enough to telephone Teresa and Kristen and then continued to cry. I held Mark's jaw shut so that when rigor mortis set in it would not be hanging open. I didn't want the girls to see him that way. Finally at half past eight, I took a shower and dressed. I also shaved Mark with his electric razor. Again I got under the feather comforter with him one last time. His body was still warm although the blood had left his face. The girls arrived at nine, and the three of us sat with him, crying and talking. I felt it was healthy for them to touch his body, to be with him and kiss him if they wanted, to remove whatever fear of death they might have. I left them alone for awhile. It was a good decision, which I realized later when I read what Kristen wrote:

> We went inside the house and directly to their bedroom. I remember pausing for a split second before entering. I was apprehensive about being so close to my dad's body, but it was important to see him. He looked so unreal. I'll always be thankful to Mom for not "shielding us" during this time. We all sat around Dad for awhile, and then Mom let us have our own time alone with him. Intellectually and philosophically, I knew that he was no longer a part of this body. It was so clearly a shell that his spirit had left behind and didn't need anymore. He was free now. But, emotionally, I was not yet ready to give up the physical body that had been with us all our lives. I needed to

hold his hand and see for myself that he was gone. I
needed this time to say good bye.

Later Ran came into the room. He needed to do something to help, so he went outside to clean off bird droppings
he had noticed on the window over the bed. The water
hammering the window right over our heads provided the
comic relief we needed and we laughed at the absurdity of
it all.

Finally it seemed time to call the funeral home to come
and get Mark's body. It had been a strong, beautiful body
and had served its purpose well as a vehicle for Mark's spirit.
But now his spirit was soaring free and Mark no longer
needed that "shell."

When the hearse rolled into our driveway, Teresa and
Kristen saw it was a metallic forest-green color, and they
tried hard not to go into another spasm of laughter. Green,
all right, but metallic? It is strange how, in deep grief, laughter and tears are so closely connected, both providing a
much-needed release.

Teresa and Kristen sat with me as we met with the
funeral director and the minister of the local Methodist
church, who had been so good about coming out to visit
often. Kristen took notes, knowing I was distracted and
wouldn't remember much.

When I told the funeral director we wanted Mark cremated, he asked about what kind of urn we wanted. Kristen,
Teresa, and I looked at each other, smiling knowingly, and
said, half under our breath, "Can-A-Man." The funeral director and minister looked somewhat shocked so I tried to
explain.

Years earlier, Mark and I were lounging around with
Bonnie and Rodney, entertaining ourselves by dreaming up
money-making schemes and new inventions. We hit on an
idea of a business that cremated people and put the ashes
into a pop-top can, like a soda can. In the event of a disas-
ter where the whole family died, their ashes could be put

into a convenient six-pack. We called this new industry "Can-A-Man" and laughed for hours as we brainstormed together the marketing and advertising slogans. No one had better ideas or more fun with this idea than Mark. Over the years, we revisited this concept off and on, making new suggestions and improvements.

We knew wherever Mark was now, he was chuckling too.

I asked the funeral director not to cremate Mark for three days. He asked why, explaining that since he didn't have refrigeration, he'd have to embalm him to do that. So, in front of our dear conservative minister, I tried to explain—not too well I'm afraid—my belief that the etheric body may take as many as three days to totally vacate the physical body. So just to cover all bases, I wanted to wait.

Deep in my heart, however, I felt Mark was free and clear of his body. I even had the image of him calling, "Clear!" just as he did before he started the engine of his airplane and then, in my mind's eye, I saw him taking off to do what he loved best—fly.

That whole day had a surreal quality. I made memorial arrangements and telephoned family members and close friends. I told my family they didn't need to come for the memorial because we would bring Mark's ashes to Minnesota for burial at Thanksgiving.

Mark and I had talked about how he would contact me after death. Now that Mark was on the other side, strange things started to happen that I believe were his way of telling us he was alive and well in spirit. The day he died, we were in the great room having pizza when we heard the toaster pop up out in the kitchen although no one had touched it. That evening I lit a candle on his bedside table while I listened to the music we were going to use for his memorial service. All at once the flame jumped about four inches above the wick and began dancing around and up and down! There was no air moving, no drafts, no reason for it to do this. When the flame finally settled down, I called Teresa and Kristen in and told them to sit on the bed, look at the candle and think of their dad. They did and very soon the flame jumped up and started to dance around again!

The next morning the phone rang once, at exactly six-thirty, the time of Mark's passing over. I answered it; the line was open but I couldn't hear anyone speaking. For several mornings after that, the phone would ring once at exactly six-thirty. It got so I didn't pick the phone up. I would just talk to Mark, knowing he could hear me. "Are you having fun yet?" I felt a little envious because now he sees and knows about all the mysteries I've wondered about for so many years. I'm happy for him. He is free to carry on with his learning. And I know he is only a prayer away.

Chapter Nineteen

Memorial Services

On Sunday afternoon we held the memorial service at the Unity Church we used to attend in Oakton, Virginia, so our friends would not have so far to drive. We had enlarged some photos of Mark at various stages of his life, even a couple baby pictures. We placed these at the entrance and in the sanctuary for friends to remember him vibrantly alive and doing things he loved.

The night before the memorial I had told Spirit, "Help me. I can't do this on my own." The next morning I felt the most incredible calm and peace—even joy. I was happy for Mark to be released from pain and to be now in a place of perfect love. We gathered to celebrate a life well lived. I found I even had the strength to comfort others.

After the opening prayer and scripture reading, our Methodist minister gave a short obituary, mentioning a few of Mark's honors and awards. He remarked how Mark had many interests, but the most important thing in his life was his family.

The hauntingly beautiful sound of the Don Cossack Singers' song filled the church. It was powerful. It didn't matter that it was sung in Russian and we didn't know what the words meant. At one time in his life Mark considered the Russians his enemy, so it was somehow fitting a Russian sing at his memorial service, a suitable reminder of the truth that we are all one and at death there is no need to understand words. After the song ended, I gave my tribute to Mark, telling how we had met in college and recognized each other as soul mates. I told them about our early life of adventure together and how grateful I was he retired at fifty, so we had ten rich years of semi-retirement together we would not have had otherwise. I continued, "Mark developed kidney cancer when he was fifty-five and of course that changed our lives dramatically. We realized each day was precious and we committed ourselves to do and say those things that were in our hearts. We did this for five and a half years."

I closed by saying, "Mark always loved a good adventure and now he is on the greatest adventure of all. He was the love of my life. As far as I was concerned, he was the best husband in the world, the best father to our daughters, and my best friend. I'm going to miss him very, very much." My voice didn't waiver until the last couple of sentences, and I thanked Spirit for giving me such incredible strength when I needed it most.

When I stepped down, Teresa took my place and with Spirit supporting her was able to give a short tribute. She had written it down as she didn't think she could give it extemporaneously:

"There is a saying that a man is known by the company he keeps. And for me, the best illustration of who my father was is embodied by all the people here today and all the people who supported him through the past five years and especially through the past few weeks.

"My father taught me many lessons throughout my life, how to tie my shoes, how to slide down a laundry shoot, how to drive and how to determine the filling in a chocolate without having to bite into it. But through the way he handled his battle with cancer, I learned the greatest lesson he had to teach—his example of grace and good humor in the face of adversity will continue to shape my life. My father told me that he would be with us even after he had gone, and there is an excerpt from a poem by George Eliot called *The Choir Invisible* that echos that sentiment:

> *Oh may I join the choir invisible*
> *Of those immortal dead who live again*
> *In minds made better by their presence:*
> *May I reach*
> *That purest heaven, be to other souls*
> *The cup of strength in some great agony,*
> *Enkindle generous ardor, feed pure love,*
> *Beget the smiles that have no cruelty,*
> *Be the sweet presence of good diffused,*
> *And in diffusion ever more intense!*
> *So shall I join the choir invisible,*
> *Whose music is the gladness of the world.*

Kristen was not sure she would be able to speak to the group because, as she says, "I cry at AT&T commercials." But Spirit was with her too. "I was always amazed at all the things my dad could do. He could fly airplanes—he had his ship captain's license—he could design and build houses—and those were just his hobbies!" She went on: "I felt there was never anything he couldn't fix or solve—or at least make a joke about. My dad was such a constant in my life that I didn't realize how much he meant to others. Looking around here at all of you and listening to everyone's stories over the past couple of weeks, I realize how deeply he did touch so many lives." Back in 1948, Kristen's uncle Ran had given Mark a copy of *The Prophet* by Kahlil Gibran, and now she read from it:

> *"Only when you drink from the river of silence shall*
> *   you indeed sing.*
> *And when you have reached the mountain top, then*
> *   you shall begin to climb.*

*And when the earth shall claim your limbs, than shall
you truly dance."*

The Unity minister opened up the service to anyone
who wanted to say something. I had not asked anyone to
prepare any remarks but friends stepped forward sponta-
neously and began to speak, freely expressing their emotions
filling the church with incredible love. Gary was the ninth
person to give a tribute and his closing remarks seemed to
summarize and reflect what others had said.

"Mark was fearless, alive, passionate, sensitive, and focused on the things that really mattered in life. He blessed
us with a unique and powerful death. I was with Mark ten
days ago, and I've been thinking about it every day since
then. I know I will remember that last time together for
the rest of my life. I'll remember the beauty that I saw
there, the Christ that I saw there, the 'all men' that I saw
there and the peace. I hope that when my time comes I can
face my death with the same fearlessness, the same love,
that Mark did and I thank Mark for showing me that is
possible."

The service had already gone on for an hour and a half.
Finally, the minister stood and told us, "This has been the
most remarkable expression of appreciation that I have ever
experienced at a memorial service in all the years I've done
them."

The tape Teresa made of *Amazing Grace* was played.
Her beautiful voice singing a cappella filled the sanctuary
and provided reflection time before the minister read the
"Traveler," by James D. Freeman and made some brief closing remarks. "It has been a humbling experience to be a
witness and to listen to the sharing from all of you. Love
resonates in this room from it. How blessed we all have
been to have had Mark as a teacher in our lives."

We followed the playing of *Taps* with a moment of silence, while everyone held a happy thought of Mark. We
closed with the Unity prayer of protection.

Friends had prepared refreshments in the vestibule and everyone stopped by for hugs and to speak of the love we were all feeling before leaving.

Since Mark's sisters were not able to be there, we'd taped the service. A week later I listened to the audiotape before sending it to them. After *Taps* was played and while the final prayer was being said, loud raucous sounds of a revelry-type music played over it all. I laughed out loud. "Now, how did Mark manage to do that?" Even if the explanation for how the wake-up music got on the new tape wasn't metaphysical, it seemed very appropriate. Mark was indeed waking up to a new life!

After that, on the tape, the pianist played a wonderful rendition of *Amazing Grace* as people were leaving the sanctuary. As I continued to listen to the tape, I wept. Looking out the open window through my tears, I saw that the wind had suddenly risen and was swirling around in the woods, building to a crescendo along with the music. Branches bent as if leaning over to talk more closely to the branches on the next tree. I had the thought they must be whispering praises of a life well lived. In the distance thunder rolled, although above there was only blue sky. How curious! And, as the song softly ended, so too did the wind. I saw silent woods standing still and strong.

A few days later, I stood looking out that same window noticing a single small leaf in the middle of the round white table on the deck. I looked up and saw another single leaf slowly swirling down in a spiral. As I watched, it gently fluttered to rest next to the other leaf, just as I somehow knew it would, side by side and slightly overlapping. Then I heard Mark's voice clearly in my head, "Yes, I am with you."

On the day of Mark's death, Kristen brought her huge cuddly teddy bear for me. The first night I spent alone in the house was a week after the memorial service. I sat on the couch hugging the very large bear as I read. It was dark out. Suddenly there was a knock on the sliding glass door, just a few feet away. The United Parcel Service man had seen lights on in the back of the house and gone to the sliding door off the deck rather than to the front door. He could see inside clearly. I'm sure he must have wondered why on earth I was sitting there hugging and reading to a stuffed bear.

Two weeks after Mark's passing, I had a dream. But it was different from any dream I'd ever had; it seemed so real! Mark was with me in bed holding me in his arms. His body was firm and strong as it had been before he'd gotten sick. I could feel his strength, and it was very loving and comforting. I wondered if I had gone to the astral level or if he had come to me on this level. I guess it doesn't matter. It was such a wonderful experience and no one can tell me it wasn't real.

Shortly after that, I was in town sleeping at Teresa's and Kristen's apartment. I had just gone to bed and was lying on my side when I felt warm air being blown into my left ear. This continued for some time. Then I remembered once months earlier when Mark and I were discussing how he would contact me after death, he had chuckled and said, "I'm going to blow into your left ear when you're making love to someone else!"

"That's not funny!" I retorted. But now, I smiled and figured Mark was fulfilling that promise, too, but not when I was with someone else. "Thank you very much for that, Mark."

We flew to Minnesota for Thanksgiving and to have a second memorial service with my family. Mark's ashes were placed in a rosewood urn and packed in a cardboard box we carried with us on the plane. Teresa was carrying it and was the first of us to go through the airport security check. I was horrified to see them ask Teresa to take the box over to the side table for examination. "What's in the box? It looks like a box of Crisco." By the time I'd grabbed my bags and gotten over to Teresa's side, she had just finished explaining what the contents were. The security person had a stricken look on her face and said, "Y'all go on ahead. I'm not gonna mess with your daddy!"

On board the plane, we found it difficult to fit the box into the overhead compartment. We could almost hear Mark saying, "See? That's another good reason for Can-A-Man!"

It was comforting to go home to the loving arms of family. I was glad we did not have to be alone for our first holiday without Mark. He had said goodbye to them just three months ago, and now it was time for the family to say their farewell to him. Deep snow lay on the ground and more was predicted, but nearly all of our family members still drove to Mother's home in Herman. We gathered for an informal service around the big table in the dining room, spilling into the kitchen and living room as well. Family members took turns sharing memories of Mark. I gazed at the faces of the children, now all sitting quietly and listening, perhaps fully comprehending what was happening.

My brother Bob is on the cemetery board for Herman, and he had dug the hole for the urn the day before, taking the soil home in buckets to keep it inside so it wouldn't freeze. That night, it snowed again and Bob was up early plowing out the road and shoveling the grave site area all over again. He even had clipped evergreen boughs for the urn to be placed on.

I linked arms with Teresa and Kristen, and we stood together and wept. I could feel family hands on our backs as Ron led us in a final prayer and read the words to *Taps*, which I had never heard before:

> *Day is done*
> *Gone the sun*
> *From the lakes*
> *From the hills*
> *From the sky.*

All is well
Safely rest
God is nigh.

There, next to the grave of my father, Aunt Mildred, and nephew John, we lovingly placed a flower beside Mark's urn before we turned to go.

That Christmas I tucked this note in my Christmas cards to friends scattered across the country who might not have heard of Mark's passing:

A Year of Transition and Transformation

Mark demonstrated that one can live with cancer without bitterness, but with great courage, good humor and peace. This past year he also showed us how to die with grace and dignity. He was surrounded by the love of friends and family and made his transition at home on November 4, 1993. If Planet Earth is our school house, Mark graduated with honors!

I plan to stay here in the house Mark built, in the woods by the river, finding great solace in nature. Teresa and Kristen live just a little over an hour away and are also my joy and comfort. Mark left a fine legacy. After 35 years of marriage, I will begin a new life. I thank you all for your prayers and support.

At Christmas we celebrate a birth to remind us there is no death. Please have a wonderful holiday filled with joy and peace, friends, family, fun, and good cheer!

It was too painful to have Christmas at the house; Mark would not be coming down the spiral staircase bedecked in his outrageous red patterned Christmas pants that he always wore. He would not be reading the Christmas story as he always did before we sang songs and opened presents. So we broke with tradition. I went to Teresa's and Kristen's apartment, and we had a very simple and quiet holiday. We tried to sing Christmas carols, but we all started to cry so we just opened presents quietly.

Chapter Twenty

Life Goes On – Forever

Five months passed. I was learning to take care of the cars and basic house maintenance and was amazed at how much I didn't know. Mark had always handled these sorts of things. I actually enjoyed making independent decisions, including remodeling the bedroom completely and creating a meditation center in it. I added white wicker rocking chairs and furniture and made the whole room more open and airy. I needed to do this because the memories of Mark dying in this room came flooding into my mind with the full force of sadness. I wanted to remember the love but release the pain. Changing the configuration of the room helped.

Two years after Mark had been diagnosed with cancer he bought me a beautiful new diamond ring to replace the small one he could afford in college. As he slipped it on my finger he said, "Whenever you look at this ring, think of me." I've gotten into the habit of kissing it every day and then sending Mark the thought, "I love you forever." I like to believe somewhere, a radiantly joyful Mark is smiling, nodding his head, and sending me back the thought, "Forever is a *verrrry* long time."

June 1994

It's been seven and a half months since Mark died. It was 100 degrees today but I still go outside to sit on the back deck, getting the energy from the woods as I did so often during Mark's illness. A mockingbird is singing, and it sounds slightly comical tonight with its trebly trills. I believe it is a gift as I don't remember mockingbirds in the woods before this year.

I remember how last year whenever I was feeling low, I'd ask the universe for a sign and I'd see a shooting star or I'd see a deer standing and grazing a few feet from our deck, or a bald eagle would swoop over the tree tops, thrilling me with the view of its majestic white head and broad wing span. This spring I was wishing I had more song birds in the woods and I was awakened the very next morning to a chorus outside my window such as I've never heard before! When I looked out there must have been over a hundred bright yellow goldfinches, all singing their little hearts out. Coincidences? I think not. After all, I've just read *Celestine Prophecy!* I ask and the universe never fails to respond.

It seems as if I've needed an inordinate amount of sleep this year and I have honored that. I don't believe it is depression. I just have a lot of battery recharging to do. I've been thinking about sharing with family parts of my journal and parts of Mark's to reflect our passage through the uncharted cancer journey. I've kept busy with other things, perhaps as a way to avoid writing about the sacred vigil, although part of me wants to do so. There will be a time when it feels right.

In the face of death, Mark continued to learn lessons—he learned to live in the present moment, to heal emotionally, to model courage and integrity, and finally, to teach that death is nothing to be feared—it is healing into spirit. Mark's personality struggled to keep the physical form alive because he didn't know consciously when his soul's mission was completed. None of us does, so we have to keep on trying to stay here as long as we can. He wanted to stay on the "other side" the first time he died as a boy, but it wasn't his time. He said when we dated that he never wanted to be old. Did he have a "knowing" or a "remembrance" of his future? We don't die too young, we die right on schedule—the soul's schedule. Perhaps his purpose in life was to teach us how to die.

My niece Donna and her husband Ron had asked Mark and me to be godparents for their son Thomas. When Mark died, they decided they still wanted us both as godparents, one in spirit and one on earth. The baptism was to be held at the Spiritual Frontiers Fellowship Retreat in Minnesota in July. I knew Mark would be present.

Once at the retreat, which was held at Carleton College, I felt Mark's presence all week. On Thursday morning, at five-thirty, the phone in our dormitory room rang once. I was rooming with my sister and niece, and Mayva picked up the receiver. The line was open but no one spoke. I thought it might be Mark again, although he had not called in several months. I was expecting him to call to let us know he would be there for the baptism. But this call was an hour early. Then suddenly I remembered I was in Minnesota and that at home in Virginia, Eastern Standard Time, it was six-thirty. I felt certain the call was from Mark, especially since it was Thursday, the day of the week on which he died. Mayva and Vicki were also convinced. No one else knew our room or our phone number. And surely no one else would have called us so early in the morning.

The next morning the phone rang again, only once and at exactly five-thirty. This time Vicki jumped up and answered it. Again, an open line but no one spoke. Mark must have had a cosmic giggle at waking all three of us again so early. That evening we said aloud, "Look, Mark we're really tired. It would be okay if you don't call again tomorrow morning."

The third morning the phone rang once again, exactly at five-thirty, but no one got up to answer it. Then I realized that neither Mayva nor Vicki heard it ring, answering a question that had been puzzling me. When I was home alone and heard that one ring, I didn't know if the phone had actually rung or if it had just rung in my head. Now I realized it could happen both ways. Apparently Mark had taken pity on them and let them sleep, but he still wanted me to know he was very much with us.

That morning at breakfast little "Thomas, Tommy, Tom," as his big brother called him, sat in his high chair and giggled and laughed out loud as though someone was playing with him while he looked off to his right and to a spot above his head. There was nothing there, but Tommy reached out his little arms, laughed, and clapped and seemed quite clearly to be seeing and playing with someone we could not see. I felt it must be Mark. Mark continued to play with him for some time and people passing by would stop and stare. Donna and Ron were happy to know their son really did have an angel by his side, his godfather in spirit.

I sat and meditated in the Japanese peace garden and again felt Mark's presence very close. I thought how Mark would love this garden and how it would be a wonderful place for the baptism that afternoon. I was not surprised when I went inside, and Ron told me that the ceremony would be held there. Mark had planned to create a Japanese garden at home but became too ill to do it. I renewed my intent to create a memorial garden dedicated to Mark when I returned to Virginia. It also became clear to me Mark wanted me to tell our story, our journey of living with cancer and facing death and his healing into spirit. It would be his gift to others to help them on their transition into spirit, and it would be my gift to bring comfort to those who are left behind.

So during the summer and fall I wrote. It was a big part of my grieving and healing process. I realized as I reread my journal how much I identified with Mark, even saying "our doctor's appointment" and "we are starting chemotherapy." Was I making his cancer mine? I am well aware of research that spouses often die shortly after the death of their loved one. I believed I wanted to live and was surprised when a person I'd just met told me that because I was so connected to Mark I had a death wish to follow him. I had gone with Teresa, Kristen, and some friends to pick apples. We were sitting on a hillside overlooking a beautiful orchard and eating a picnic lunch, when a woman with piercing blue eyes sat beside me and calmly told me that she was from beyond the Pleiades and that I had work to do but first I had to decide if I wanted to live. She led me through a process that was so engrossing we were oblivious to the others. They went apple picking without us. I don't even remember exactly what she said or what happened but I believe that it was at this point that I reinstated my desire to live.

I encouraged Teresa and Kristen to write about their feelings too. Teresa wrote of her pain and of her learnings:

I knew it was going to hurt to lose Dad, but I didn't know that meant literal pain. I felt a real, physical pain in my heart area, giving a totally new meaning to phrases like "heartache." The pain was incredible, but even then, I was aware that something awesome was happening. For as he started to let go, to give himself over to what was happening, there was a kind of peace that I could see and feel.

I could also see it on the faces of the people who came to be with him in the final days. This look of peace and wonderment underneath the tears and sorrow. For as his physical body shrank away, his spirit became more evident. Without the distraction of the personality that had been Mark Peterson, this shining soul came shining through.

It was a life-altering time for me. I started to question so many of my beliefs and "truths." Goals and ambitions of success that had driven me for so long now seemed hollow and meaningless.

I was devastated, but for the first time in my life I met the pain head on rather than hiding or trying to distract myself. And when the pain got to be too bad to bear, I gave up trying to do it myself and turned it over to God.

That's when the light appeared at the end of the tunnel. I am no where near out of the tunnel yet, but I am well on my way. My dad showed me the way to live by how he approached his death. And if I can live with even a fraction of the courage, grace, strength, and humor with which he died I will consider myself lucky.

Even now I feel him with me often. It's almost as if I turn my head fast enough, I will be able to catch a glimpse of him standing just off to the side—watching, guiding, and protecting, just like always.

Exactly one year after we buried Mark's ashes, we dedicated a Japanese garden to his memory. I shared the symbolism with friends and family gathered. It is all here—the path that has no beginning and no end—because we walked together before this lifetime and we will walk together again after this lifetime.

The plants that know when to bloom and when to fade, true to their own blueprint. Mark had his own blueprint, his own sealed orders, as we all do. Once here we don't remember what the soul agreed to experience in this lifetime, but Mark's soul knew when his work was completed and when it was time to go home.

The water flows through a bamboo pipe fountain into a hollowed out basin of the rock below, spilling over the edge making a lovely babbling sound. The living, loving, flowing waters of Spirit that we can't push, can't change, can't stop the flow without it becoming stagnant. All we can do is to go with the flow. In dying Mark learned this lesson, to "let go and let god." His final stage of acceptance had led him to peaceful waters. Teresa and Kristen each added a special stone to the basin to signify their dad will always be a part of them.

The lantern is symbolic of the divine light within all of us, the light that connects us all together. Whenever we think a loving thought of Mark, we send a spark of that divine light back out into the universe. Indeed, lots of little sparks flew out to another dimension that day as friends lit a candle of remembrance, and smudged sweet grass and juniper berries. We closed our dedication ceremony by singing *Amazing Grace* together, substituting the word wretch with "to save a *soul* like me." God does not think we are wretches and we shouldn't either.

Holding this little ritual ceremony in the garden on the first year anniversary of Mark's burial somehow brought a sense of closure for me. I do not expect Mark to hang around as he has things to learn and places to go. I bless him on his way into other dimensions. I don't want to keep him earth bound, nor do I really believe I can. Somehow, too, I no longer think of him as my husband now but more as a very old and beloved soul I've known before and will know again. Mark's life did not end. That would be impossible because life is eternal. He just dropped the body. Death here in our physical dimension is birth in the spiritual realm—birth into an enlivened energetic essence. All Mark really lost was limitation. Now he can truly dance. I'll catch up to him later!

Epilogue

One morning, a year after Mark died, the phone rang at six-thirty rousing me from a deep sleep. I had grown accustomed to Mark's signal he was with me in spirit, but this time it was different. I felt the urge to pick up my journal and write. Since I'm not a morning person I was scarcely aware of the words I scrawled down on paper. When it seemed finished, I put the notebook down and went back to sleep. Later in the morning I read the message that began with "Blessings and good day." It seemed to be from Mark.

The phone has continued to wake me often at exactly six-thirty in the morning; when it does I write, with my eyes barely open, and read later words of hope, comfort, and promise. I can't prove the messages come from Mark rather than my own subconscious—and I don't feel a need to convince anyone. It is comforting for me to believe Mark is communicating.

A Message From Mark

Blessings and good day. Yes, I am with you. You feel my presence. It is so beautiful here you would not wish me there. There is no remorse, no regrets—I am free and unbounded. It is a state of joy you would not deny anyone.

Grief moves us to do and say things that then can help others. The book is a case in point. Others cannot share the experience with you—as each person's pain is theirs alone—but they can empathize with the emotions common and known to all. Write and I will fly with it.

I chose cancer so I'd have the time to work through earthly issues and re-remember gradually. Cancer is a learning tool. Death is something everyone has to face. So talk about it. Not everyone will be healed physically—but all are healed in spirit. The learning is: do not fear death. We have to face our fears to know they are illusion.

Perhaps people do not fear death as much as they fear judgment. Were they good enough—will they make it into heaven? Lose the fear! God is love. You are love and loved. There is only joy.

Morning dawns upon the planet and in the stillness there is an expectancy, poised on the cusp of something big, not knowing what it is. Time has come for changes to be made on a planetary level. The end of an era—the beginning of a new phase in the great experiment. Fortify yourself with love and intentions of union. Union—it is a wonderful word and a beautiful reality. Rest in the knowing that it is all according to divine plan.

Resources

Cancer Information Service at National Cancer Institute 1-800-4-cancer, request "PDQ" to get latest information on treatment for each type of cancer.

Commonweal, P.O. Box 316, Bolinas, CA 94924, (415) 868-0970, Michael Lerner, Ph.D., president. Offers several publications, a guide to alternative and adjunctive cancer therapies, and cancer help programs.

Institute for Attitudinal Studies, P.O. Box 19222, Alexandria, VA 22320-0222, (703) 706-5333, Susan Trout, Ph.D., Executive Director. Non-profit organization which provides support groups, facilitation and study groups.

Books

A Course in Miracles. Tiburon, CA: Foundation for Inner Peace, 1975.

A Gift of Healing: Selections from A Course in Miracles. Los Angeles: Jeremy P. Tarcher, Inc. 1988.

Bietz, Dorien. *Unbound: A Spiritual Guide to Mastery of the Material World.* Reston, VA: Entity Press, 1986.

Borysenko, Joan. *Minding the Body, Mending the Mind* Menlo Park, CA: Addison-Wesley Publishing, 1987.

Brown, Virginia with Susan Stayman. *Macrobiotic Miracle.* New York: Japan Publication, 1984.

Bryant, Barry. *Cancer and Consciousness*. Boston: Sigo Press, 1990.

Cousins, Norman. *The Healing Heart*. New York: Avon, 1983.

Dacher, Elliott S., M.D. *PNI: The New Mind/Body Healing Program*. New York: Paragon House, 1991.

Doctors Look at Macrobiotics. Edited by Edward Esko, New York: Japan Publications, 1988.

Dossey, Larry, M.D. *Beyond Illness*. Boulder, CO: New Science Library, Shambala Publications, 1984.

Epstein, Gerald, M.D. *Healing Visualizations: Creating Health Through Imagery*. New York: Bantam Books, 1989.

Esko, Edward, editor. *Doctors Look at Macrobiotics*. New York: Japan Publications, 1988.

Fawcett, Ann, and Cynthia Smith. *Cancer-Free: 30 Who Triumphed Over Cancer Naturally*. New York: Japan Publications, 1991.

Jampolsky, Gerald G., M.D. *Love Is Letting Go of Fear*. Millbrae, CA: Celestial Arts, 1979.

_____. *Teach Only Love*. New York: Bantam Books, 1983.

Kübler-Ross, Elisabeth. *On Death and Dying*. New York: Collier Books, Macmillan, 1974.

_____. *To Live Until We Say Good-Bye; Death: The Final Stage of Growth*. Englewood Cliffs, NJ: Prentice-Hall, 1978.

Kushi, Michio with Alex Jack. *The Cancer Prevention Diet*. New York: St. Martin's Press, 1983.

Kushi, Michio. *Cancer and Heart Disease: The Macrobiotic Approach to Degenerative Disorders*. New York: Japan Publications, 1995.

LeShan, Lawrence. *You Can Fight for Your Life*. New York: M. Evans and Co.

_____. *Cancer as a Turning Point*. Plume. 1994.

Levine, Stephen. *Healing into Life and Death*. New York: Doubleday, 1987.

Moody, R. *Life After Life*. New York: Bantam, 1975.

_____. *Reunions: Visionary Encounters with Departed Loved Ones*. New York: Villard Books, 1993.

Moss, Richard, M.D. *The I That Is We: Awakening to Higher Energies Through Unconditional Love*. Millbrae, CA: Celestial Arts, 1981.

Ornstein, Robert, and David Sobel. *The Healing Brain*. New York: Simon and Schuster, 1987.

Pelletier, Kenneth R. *Mind as Healer, Mind as Slayer*. New York: Dell Publishing, 1977.

Redfield, James. *The Celestine Prophecy*. Hoover, AL: Satori Publishing, 1993.

_____. *The Tenth Insight*. New York: Warner Books, 1996.

Ring, Kenneth. *Heading Toward Omega: In Search of the Meaning of Near-Death Experience*. New York: Quill/William Morrow and Co., 1985.

Sattilaro, Anthony, M.D. *Recalled by Life*. New York: Avon Books, 1982.

Siegel, Bernie S., M.D. *Love, Medicine and Miracles*. New York: Harper and Row Publishers, 1986.

_____. *Peace, Love and Healing*. New York: Harper and Row Publishers, 1989.

Simonton, O. Carl, M.D. and Stephanie Matthews Simonton. *Getting Well Again*. Los Angeles: Jeremy P. Tarcher, 1979.

Stevenson, Ian. *Children Who Remember Previous Lives*. Charlottesville, VA: University Press of Virginia, 1987.

_____. *Twenty Cases Suggestive of Reincarnation*. Charlottesville, VA: University Press of Virginia, 1966.

_____. *Unlearned Language.*Charlottesville, VA: University Press of Virginia, 1984.

Trout, Susan, *To See Differently.* Washington, D.C.: Three Roses Press, 1990.

Wilber Ken, *Grace and Grit.* Boston: Shambhala Publications, 1991.

Worrall, Ambrose with Olga Worrall. *The Gift of Healing.* New York: Harper and Row, 1965.

Give the Gift of
Comfort and Inspiration
to Your Friends and Loved Ones

CHECK YOUR LEADING BOOKSTORE OR ORDER HERE

YES, I want _____ copies of *Love Has No Fear* at $12.95 each, plus $3 shipping per book (Virginia residents please add .58 state sales tax per book). Canadian orders must be accompanied by a postal money order in U.S. funds. Allow 15 days for delivery.

My check or money order for $_____ is enclosed.
Please charge my: ❑ Visa ❑ MasterCard

Name _____

Organization _____

Phone _____

Address _____

City/State/Zip _____

Card #_____ Exp. Date _____

Signature _____

Please make your check payable and return to:
Merkaba Press
P.O. Box 6511
Falls Church, VA 22040
Call your credit card order to: (800) 673-6056

All proceeds from the sale of this book
will be used to provide dolphin experiences
for children with cancer.